FORMULA ONE
FAMOUS FAILURES

Matthew Teaters

Order this book online at www.trafford.com/08-1038
or email orders@trafford.com

Most Trafford titles are also available at major online book retailers.

Edited by Matthew Teaters.
Cover Design/Artwork by Vanessa Teaters.
Photography by Vanessa Teaters.
Note for Librarians: A cataloguing record for this book is available from Library
and Archives Canada at www.collectionscanada.ca/amicus/index-e.html

Printed in the United States of America.

ISBN: 978-1-4251-8528-2 (sc)

Trafford Rev. date: 06/27/2011

 www.trafford.com

North America & international
toll-free: 1 888 232 4444 (USA & Canada)
phone: 250 383 6864 ♦ fax: 250 383 6804 ♦ email: info@trafford.com

The United Kingdom & Europe
phone: +44 (0)1865 487 395 ♦ local rate: 0845 230 9601
facsimile: +44 (0)1865 481 507 ♦ email: info.uk@trafford.com

10 9 8 7 6 5 4 3 2

Matthew David Teaters

April 5, 1982 – December 10, 2004

Matthew was sick from the first day he was born. Even though he suffered all his life he dedicated his life to taking care of others. He was a wonderful Christian and never met a stranger. He was always going to church, visiting the sick in hospitals in nursing homes and helping anyone that he could. His greatest loves were the Lord and racing. He taught himself to read by reading racing magazines and loved every minute of it. Matthew wrote for a Formula One Column on the internet. His great love is this book. We hope you will enjoy reading the book as much as he enjoyed writing it. He put his whole heart into it. Even though he suffered his whole life he was on the national dean's list for his writing.

He was our hero and will always be. He was taken from us so early in life but the Lord needed him more.

Please enjoy his book for his memory. We just wish he could have known how much it pleased others.

We love and miss him,

Your family

FORMULA ONE FAMOUS FAILURES

Created in 1950, the Formula One World Championship is the pinnacle of auto racing. The most popular form of motor sports on Earth, some of its marquee teams are known throughout the world, such as Ferrari, McLaren, and Lotus. Formula One's glamorous outlook and incredible marketing power make one believe that it is a fantasy world of expensive machinery and super hero drivers, a dazzling array of lines and colors. But if one looks closer into the history of the world Championship, one will notice another side to Formula one, a side of failure. It is obvious that not every car can be a Lotus 49 or a Williams FW 14B. And not every engine can have the impact of a Ford Cosworth DFV or a Honda turbo, in fact very few are, but some stand out as some of Formula One's most famous failures. What are the worst? That is certainly open to debate. Each year, for every winner, there are numerous disappointments, but this novel hopes to illustrate the fights and famines of the Grand Prix World.

TABLE OF CONTENTS

1950 CLEMENTE BIONDETTI

Chassis: Ferrari 166T
Engine: Jaguar XK in-line 6, 3.4-liter normal aspiration
Best Result: DNF (Biondetti, Italy)

THE 2000 SEASON is generally regarded as the first time that a Formula One car bearing the name Jaguar has taken its place on the grid. That is not totally true, for in 1950, Clemente Biondetti took a Jaguar engine derived from Le Mans and matted it with his Ferrari. The ultimate "odd couple", indeed.

Clemente Biondetti had a rather successful racing career leading up to the break in motorsports caused by World War II. He won the famous Mille Miglia in an Alfa Romeo 2900B and after the end of World War II, he again won the prestigious Italian road race in 1947, again in Alfa Romeo 2900B. He then went on to win two more Mille Miglias in 1948 and 49, both times driving for Ferrari.

By 1950, he was driving for Jaguar in a C-type at Le Mans when at the same time; the Formula One Championship had been formed. Eager to compete in his home Grand Prix in Italy, Biondettihe lifted the Jaguar XK engine and gearbox out of the Jaguar and put it in the Ferrari 166T (which was most likely from the basis of a Maserati) that he owned. Also borrowed from the Jaguar were the gearbox, front suspension, brakes, and transmission. With these modifications, Biondetti created the odd Ferrari-Jaguar. The entrant bore his own name, and the organizers gave him the number 22.

He qualified 25th out of the 27 starters, but Paul Pietsch's Maserati's didn't record a qualifying time so he was actually next to slowest, in front of the Maserati/Milano of Franco Comotti. He was also 32 seconds off the pole time of Juan Manual Fangio in the Alfa Romeo.

Biondetti lasted only 17 laps before the Jaguar left him down. Disappointed, he would never again attempt a Grand Prix. The Ferrari-Jaguar would be revamped with bodywork from a Spider Corsa and raced in sports cars. Biondetti then went back to the Jaguar Mille Miglia effort, before giving that up to race for Ferrari in sports cars. Biondetti finished fourth in his final Mille Miglia effort while driving for Ferrari in 1954 and would retire from racing to concentrate on battling cancer, for which he was suffering from.

Cancer claimed his life on February 24th, 1955. He was 56 years old. But he is responsible for Jaguar's first venture into Formula One, although it was hardly a Jaguar project.

1955 SCUDERIA LANCIA

Chassis: Lancia D50
Engine: Lancia DS50 V8, 2.5-liter normal aspiration
Best Result: 2nd (Castellotti, Monaco)

LOST POTENTIAL. PERHAPS that is the best way to describe the Lancia F1 project. The Lancia D50 had undoubted speed, top drivers, and a good team. So what went wrong? A combination of tragedy and economics put an end to the program in 1955, but the cars themselves would see more glory in the future under the Scuderia Ferrari.

Vincenzo Lancia had started a small, Italian car company in 1906 and yet had not seriously entered a dedicated project in motorsport, instead finding it more important to concentrate on the production car market. When he died the company was left to his son, Gianni, who did have aspirations to have the company involved in motorsports. Soon the beautiful and revolutionary Aurelia Grand Turismo sports car was hitting the tracks with its in-board rear brakes and production spec V6 engine.

But Lanica had one eye on Formula One. And soon a Lanica would be built to compete on the Grand Prix circuits. Despite Lancia being a generally small company, their Formula One effort was to be first class. Vittorio Jano had joined the company in 1937 and would oversee the work done on the F1 car, dubbed the "D50". The D50 had many innovative features. For one, it was one the first Grand Prix car to use the engine as a stressed member of the chassis. This meant that instead of simply being dropped into the car, it would now become a load-bearing member of the chassis, with only a tubular frame running underneath the engine, as the car would virtually fall apart when the engine was removed! The engine that would demonstrate this technique would be Lancia's DS50 90-degree 2.5-liter V8, which produced approximately 250 horsepower at 8,100 RPMs using dual overhead camshafts. It was also fitted into the D50 at an angle with the propeller shaft directed to the left of the driver using transaxle input gears. Another aspect of the car that was innovative was its twin fuel tanks that ran down the sides of the machine in-between the wheels. This concept would allow for better weight distribution during the races when fuel was being consumed. In addition, it also helped to clean up the "dirty air" that existed between the wheels. The car featured a five-speed gearbox and was very light in comparison with many of its competitors, weighing in at a reputed 620 kilograms. In keeping with the Italian theme, tires were supplied by the Pirelli company. The team had also made headlines by signing the legendary Alberto Ascari away from Ferrari, who officially signed on January 1st, 1954, to drive for the team.

It would make its testing debut in January of 1954 at the Casella Aerodrome but for a variety of reasons, some mechanical, some political, it wouldn't be ready until the final Grand Prix of the season when it would compete against the likes of Maserati, Ferrari, and most notably, the W196 of Mercedes-Benz who were returning to Grand Prix action for the first time since World War II. Ascari was briefly put on a loan to Maserati and then took a loaned Ferrari to the front row at Monza. In the race, Ascari had a duel with the private Maserati of Sterling Moss, only to retire after 49 laps with engine trouble. Moss then retired, giving Fangio's Mercedes yet another victory.

With the red paint barley dry, two Lancia D50s were entered for the season ending Spanish Grand Prix, one for Ascari, the other for fellow Italian Luigi Villoresi. Ascari won the pole as he was nearly a second faster than the Mercedes of Juan Fangio while Villoresi turned a respectable lap for the fifth qualifying position. Villoresi fell out after only two laps in the race after suffering brake problems while Ascari set fastest lap while leading until succumbing to clutch failure on lap ten.

But the performance was there, and many expected an all out war between Lancia and Mercedes in 1955.

For 1955, Mercedes had added Sterling Moss to partner Juan Fangio, a dream team of sorts for the German effort. So, who would be on pole for the much-anticipated battle in the 1955 season opener in Argentina? Neither Lancia nor Mercedes. Jose Froilan Gonzalez, driving Ferrari's 625 with an inline four, took pole position a half a second ahead of Ascari with Fangio's Mercedes in third. The two other Lancias, belong to Villoresi and Eugenio Castellotti, qualified in the 11th and 12th positions respectively. Villoresi had an accident on the second lap while Ascari did the same after 21 laps. Castellotti drove the number 36 Lancia for 20 circuits before handing the car over to Villoresi, who would crash on lap 36. All in all, it wasn't a great day for Lancia as Fangio's Mercedes completed all 96 grueling laps on the Argentine track to take the victory.

Acari took out his frustrations in March by beating the Ferrari and Maserati teams in the non-championship at the Turin GP and in May at the Naples GP. Three Lancias also finished in the top six at Pau. But these were generally minor events in which the Mercedes team, the real competition for Lancia, elected not to compete. Only by the Monaco Grand Prix would the Lancia be able to challenge the german opposition. Fangio took the pole around the tight and twisty circuit, and the Lancias proved to be quick as Ascari took the outside pole with Castellotti in fourth while Villoresi lined-up seventh. Louis Chiron was 19th in a fourth Lancia.

The Mercedes of Fangio took the lead from pole and eventually lead the first 49 laps before a transmission failure. The lead was then inherited by teammate Moss in the sister W196 but Ascari was catching the young Englishman. Moss held the lead until encountering engine problems on lap 81. Had he taken another lap, Ascari would have taken the lead. But almost immediately he lost control of his D50 at the swimming pool corner and his Lancia was flipped into the harbor! Although everyone feared the worst, before long the blue helmet of Ascari appeared on the surface. Ascari boarded a boat and was taken to a nearby hospital, suffering from only a broken nose and, understandably, shock at what had occurred. The Ferrari of Trintignant went to victory 20 seconds ahead of the Lancia of Castellotti. Lancia's also finished fifth and sixth as Villoresi and Chiron made it to the finish.

Whatever hope this might have caused would soon end. Alberto Ascari, seen as the man who would carry the team to the top, would lose his life in a mysterious accident in Monza just four days later. Ascari was recovering from the Monaco accident and kept busy by watching practice for the Supercortemaggiore race. Ascari was apparently ready to return home to his wife when he decided to test the new Ferrari sports car of his friend and teammate Castellotti. Ascari was in casual ware, only shirtsleeves, trousers, and borrowing Castellotti's helmet. On the third lap, the Ferrari skidded and then turned on its nose, barrel rolling twice. Ascari was catapulted out of the car onto the Monza pavement.

No one is sure about the cause of the accident, but a tire failure is suspected. Although thought to be alive directly after the accident, Ascari died a few minutes later.

Ascari was always an extremely superstitious man, and to add to this, Acari, just as his father Antonio, died on the 26th day of a month, at the age of 36, at the exit of a left hand corner, four days after walking away from an accident. It was also the superstition of many drivers' to not wear another drivers helmet.

This devastated the Lancia factory. So much so that three days after Ascari's funeral, the team officially suspended its racing operations. Although three cars were originally entered for the Belgian Grand Prix, but only Castellotti drove in what was virtually a privateer effort. Castellotti, took pole on the daunting Spa track, only to fall out of the race with gearbox problems while running third after 16 laps.

In addition, the company was under tremendous financial strain and the expensive racing operation certainly wasn't helping matters. This is why; by the summer of 1955 the family had sold the business to an investment group headed by Carlo Presenti and Fiat owner Agnelli. It was through the efforts of many parties, Fiat included, that Lanica turned over all their Grand Prix possessions to Enzo Ferrari in

July of 1995 as the Enzo claimed that he could no longer fund his racing team. This included six cars, engines, spares, team transporters, blueprints, driver Castellotti, and designer Jano, who joined the Ferrari team as a consultant. A five-year subsidy with Fiat was also arranged. It is said that one D50 remained in the hands of Gianni Lancia after the heart breaking loss of the racing effort.

With the management of the Ferrari, the Lancia D50 was finally proved a worthy design. Two Lancia-Ferraris were entered in the season ending Italian Grand Prix for Nino Farina and Villoresi. Farina qualified fifth while Villoresi lined up eight, both on a par with their Ferrari brethren's 555 in-line fours, but neither car would start the race as concerns grew in light of the cars switching from Pirelli to Englebert tires on the daunting Monza banking. The last time the cars would see action as true Lancias occurred when Mike Hawthorn had a wonderful race in Oulton Park, where he finished a strong second behind the Maserati of Moss.

Nothing was to stop the Lancia-Ferrari combination in 1956. Following the departure of Mercedes at the end of 1955 in wake of the Le Mans tragedy. Frangio joined Ferrari and along with Peter Collins, dominated the 1956 season as Fangio held off Moss to win his second consecutive title. The 1956 D50s were slightly modified from their Lancia days, as the fuel tank had been moved from the sides to the more standard position behind the driver. Other modifications to both the front and rear suspension included the tubular shock absorbers replaced with Houdaille lever-arm shock absorbers with the addition of a new anti-roll bar. The cars were dubbed the "D50A"s for the 1956 season, "A" standing for ameliorato, or improved, but eventually took on the Ferrari 801 badge.

What might have been? That is a question we will always ask. What would have became of Lancia had Ascari not been killed in Monza? What if they hadn't been forced to leave Formula One? The fact that the Ferrari team had so much success with the D50 proves that the design and passion were with Lancia, but fate and resources were not.

1956 AUTOMOBILES BUGATTI

Chassis: Bugatti T251
Engine: Bugatti in-line 8, 2.5 liter normal aspiration
Best Result: DNF (Trintignant, France)

FOR ALL THEIR success before the Second World War, it is somewhat surprising that Bugatti have a total of one World Championship race to their credit since the start of the modern era in 1950. That one race came with the unusual type 251. High hopes lead to disappointment for this legendary French manufacturer.

Ettore Bugatti was born on September 15th, 1881, the youngest son of Carlo Bugatti, a furniture designer as well as an artist. It wasn't long before Ettore was bitten by the racing bug, and became the Chief Engineer of the Deutz Company when he was just 25 years old. But this wasn't enough for Bugatti, and by 1909 he had raised the funds to start his own car company in an old dye factory at Molsheim.

People first took notice of the talented young man when his cars swept the top four finishing positions at the Voiturette Grand Prix in 1921. Despite the success, his cars were soon overtaken by bigger operations until 1924 when he designed the machine that would cement the Bugatti name as a legend, the Type 35. The Type 35 dominated racing from 1927 until 1931, and the blue French cars were some of the most famous racing machines ever built in addition to being a popular road car.

There was turmoil when Would War II broke out, as the Italian Bugatti was expected to side with Germany. In an unusual move, Bugatti purchased the La Licorne car company to design small vehicles when the war ended. After the war, the French Government accused Bugatti of treason and confiscated his factory. Just days before his death in 1947, the company was handed back to the Bugatti family.

The company was then handed down to his son, Roland. Although there had been a halfhearted attempt at a Grand Prix car with the T73C, the company was not to build a Grand Prix car that would enter the Formula One World Championship until 1956, with their unusual T251.

The project was one full of hopes and enthusiasm. The Formula One effort was intended to launch the French company into the world of luxury sport cars. Monsieur Bolore (who had made his name in cigarette papers) had married Ettore's widow and would set up the team, with funding to be supplied by the French Military.

The Type 251 and its straight 8 engine were designed by Italian Gioacchino Colombo, who had experince with Alfa Romeo, Ferrari, and Maserati (for which he designed the famous 250F). The most unusual feature of the mid-engine car was that its straight 8 cylinder engine was laid out transversely in the flat chassis, effectively making two fours arranged end-to-end. This was in an effort to improve the balance and firing order of the engine to suit each circuit. The engine was intended to produce approximately 270 at 9500 RPMs, but in reality it fell short of this target. The car also featured bulky sidepods, which housed the two fuel tanks. The famous "B" Bugatti horseshoe grill was also a prominent feature on the new car.

The work on the car was slow. Funding for the project had started to run out following the French Militarie's defeat at Dien Bien Phu and their withdraw from Vietnam. Only in November of 1955 did a prototype reach the press. Although the cars were far from ready for competition, political pressure from the company's management meant that the cars would be entered for the French Grand Prix at Reims in 1956. The driver of choice was Maurice Trintignant, the Frenchman who had been put on loan from Vanwall.

The Bugatti team had conducted a testing session at Reims in the week prior to the Grand Prix. A second car, with a longer wheelbase and some minor bodywork alterations, was constructed, but the new machine handled poorly and Trintignant reverted back to the older car fitted with the new machine's engine.

The new Bugatti's caused quite a stir in the paddock, but in reality their performance during the weekend was nothing to cause alarm. Trintignat could qualify only 18th in the 20-car field, out running only the Gordini of Andre Pilette and the private Maserati of Andre Simon. Similar mediocrity was performed in the race until Trintignant fell out with a faulty throttle pedal after only 18 laps.

By this time, the funding for the effort was nearly used up. Although both cars were returned to Molsheim for further development, it was soon apparent that the money to run them was not there. Plans to build a full fleet of Bugattis (including six Grand Prix cars and a Le Mans effort) fell through. The effort ended there. Trintignant went back to Vanwall for the remainder of the season while Bugatti itself was acquired in 1966 by Hispano-Suiza and today is part of the Volkswagen/Audi conglomerate. The cars themselves were passed onto the Schlumpf collection and now are part of the French National Collection in Mullhouse.

1959 LEADER CARDS INC.

Chassis: Kurtis Kraft Midget
Engine: Offenhauser in-line 4, 1.7-liter normal aspiration
Best result: DNF (Ward, USA)

IN THE OLD days, it was not uncommon for cars of a lower formula to be updated to Grand Prix specs and raced. The last time this occurred was in 1988 when Dallara entered an updated F3000 chassis for Alex Caffi in the Brazilian Grand Prix. However, one of the more bizarre cars to have entered a Grand Prix through the years has to be the Kurtis Kraft Midget racer with an Indianapolis style Offenhauser engine.

After years of having a Formula One race in name only, 1959 was to be the first "real" United States Grand Prix. From 1950 to 1960, the Indy 500 counted as a Formula One race. This would allow for unusual results as the Indy 500 winner would usually finish in the top ten in points despite running just one race! Except for the occasional exception, the Formula One regulars never took part in the Indy 500 and likewise rarely did the Indy 500 runners ever take part in a Grand Prix. But that would change in 1959, as Sebring had been selected to hold the first United States Grand Prix. The United States was well represented by US drivers such as Phil Hill and Harry Schell, but one entry you may not remember is that of Roger Ward in a midget car. Ward actually held a Formula One victory to his name thanks to winning the Indy 500 just a few months before, but after some convincing, took up the chance to race in the first United States Grand Prix at Sebring.

The car that Ward was to enter was an 11 year-old Kurtis Kraft midget racer, and was made for dirt racing, not asphalt. Bob Wilke owned the car as well as the Leader Cards Company, thus the entrants name would bear the name of the greeting card manufacturer. The car had two forward gears and a two-speed rear-end. Like other midgets, this car used a break leaver rather than a pedal to stop the car. The Firestone tires were mounted on 12-inch wheels. The torsion bar suspension was also adjusted to allow for left and right turns. The Offenhauser, or "Offy", engine was an in-line four cylinder that had dominated Indianapolis for years, but was not designed for road racing, particularly not for Formula One. It was downsized to 1.7 liters to conform to the Formula One regulations, and had a terrible rev range; not surprising considering it was made for oval track racing. It was modified to run Avgas rather than methanol.

The Midget was shaken down at on USAC-sanctioned Formula Libre races at Lime Rock Park and Watkins Glen. Although scoffed at by the European Community at first glance, Ward, along with other midgets, which were entered by names such as Tony Bettenhausen, Russ Klar, Brett Brooks, and Duane Carter, were to quickly show that the midget was no joke. The Watkins Glen event in particular was to give Ward a reason for hope, not because of the results of his machine, but from that of another midget. Although Sterling Moss won the race, what stood out was that the second place car driven by Eddie Johnson at the wheel of his Jerry Zello midget, which had, with the exception of Moss, been the fastest car on the track despite the pouring rain, sleet, and even at times, snow.

When Ward set out for practice in the United States Grand Prix, the car sported the number one. Today, we think of the number one as being reserved for the reigning champion, but in those days it was up to the organizers of the event to pass out numbers to the teams. Not surprisingly in this American event, the American organizers felt that Ward should have the number.

The midget was not a great car to have in any Formula One event, but at the bumpy, rough surface of the former airfield in Sebring, it was a particularly bad car. Ward qualified last, nearly 44 seconds off the pole time of Sterling Moss's Cooper Climax. He then struggled in the race, being lapped several times before finally falling out of the race with clutch problems after 20 laps around the Florida circuit.

The midget was a failure and was never in competition again. Ward would have one more go around at the 1963 US Grand Prix at Watkins Glen in a Lotus BRM but failed to make an impression and never competed in F1 again.

What Ward discovered is that racing really is apples and oranges. What is good in one form of racing may not be good in another. In fairness to Ward, it is hard to tell if Formula One cars racing on dirt would have done any better.

1963 AUTOMOBILI TURISMO E SPORT

Chassis:	ATS 100
Engine:	ATS V8, 1.5-liter normal aspiration
Best Result:	11th (Hill, Italy)

AT FIRST GLANCE, life at Enzo Ferrari's team should have been wonderful for Phil Hill during the early 1960s. Hill had won the 1961 World Championship and Baghetti had won in his first Grand Prix start in France the same year. But as often happens in Grand Prix racing, success is not enough. Bad circumstances resulted in inter-team turmoil and by the end of the 1962 season, both drivers and six team personal were on their way out of the Italian team and into a new effort known as the Automobili Turismo e Sport, better know as ATS The team was a failure, and a sad ending to many previously successful relationships.

The year is 1961. After a year of trying to resist the rear engine movement, Ferrari finally adapt and unveil the Ferrari 156 "skarknose" designed by Carlo Chiti, powered by a 1.5-liter V6. The car is striking, both in its physical appearance and its speed on the track. Driving this beast will be German Wolfgang Von Trips, Americans Ritchie Ginther and Phil Hill, and Italian Giancarlo Baghetti who would drive an occasional fourth works Ferrari. The cars were dominant in the new 1.5-liter engine formula, usually winning easily against the BRM and Lotus teams who were not prepared.

In a year where he also won the 24 Hours of Le Mans and the 12 Hours of Sebring, Hill would clinch the championship on the same day that Von Trips would lose his life in Monza, the home of the Tifosi.

This was a blow to the team, and distention began to break up the team when team manager Romolo Tavoni was asked not to attend the funeral of Von Trips, a driver that he had tremendous admiration for. Going in his place would be Franco Gozzi and Laura Ferrari, wife of Enzo Ferrari.

In fact, Laura Ferrari, who was becoming an increasingly frequent visitor to the team's factory, was one of the many circumstances that would soon shake up the team. Mrs. Ferrari had been a shareholder in Ferrari S.p.A. for years but only since 1960 had she taken an active role in the team. Many of the top team members found her presence distracting, an overbearing figure that hovered over the team and was quick to point out any shortcomings. Finally in October of 1961 just after the funeral of Von Trips, several team members wrote a letter to Enzo Ferrari suggesting that it would be best if Laura did not visit the factory. Ferrari was enraged, and before long much of the Scuderia's infrastructure found themselves on the bad side of the Italian team.

As a result, eight members of the team, including Tavoni and Chiti, left. It didn't take long for these highly sought after free agents to find work. A group of businessmen including Count Giovanni Volpi di Misturi (who had also left Ferrari), metallurgist Jaime Ortiz Patino and textile guru Ortiz Giorgio Billi, picked up the group, hoping to elevate their small sports car building company. The team formed what would be called the Societa per Azioni Automobili Turismo e Sport Serenissima. Shortly thereafter, Volpi di Misturi left, taking the Serenissima name and his substantial funding with him. The remaining members chaged the name to Automobili Turismo e Sport, or ATS. The team would be based in Bologna, Italy, a short drive away from Maranello and the Ferrari headquarters.

Hill had found the 156 less competitive in 1962, although he did have a classic Monaco drive coming from 9th to finish a fine 2nd. But the growing tension between the American and Ferrari meant that he would move to the ATS team in 1963 along with Ginacarlo Baghetti.

The first ATS 100 was completed and shown to the press in late 1962. The car looked somewhat like a Ferrari, but had very low lying nose and a high engine cover, which suggested a taller engine, although this aspect of the car would eventually be replaced with a smaller cover. It was overall a sleek, impressive car with shining aluminum bodywork. A design that drew high expectations simply from the men behind it. Chiti had developed a 90-degree, quad-overhead cam, all-aluminum V8, unlike the tiny V6 that he had worked for Ferrari; the gearbox was a modified Colotti 6-speed, mounted between the engine and the differential casing. The English Dunlop Company supplied the tires.

An intensive testing program began in early 1963. Test driver Jack Fairman conducted the initial work before Hill and Baghetti took over. From the beginning, it was clear that the ATS was dreadfully slow and hard to control compared to the Lotus and BRM teams. The engine was underpowered and underdeveloped, as well as having a reputation for frequent oil leaks.

ATS was way behind schedule, despite stating the previous year. The team never contested any of the early season non-Championship races and never showed up for the first round of the season in Monaco, despite the organizers reserving the starting-numbers 1 and 2 for the duo. Not exactly the idea showing for a group that was thought to have "super team" potential.

When the team finally made it to Spa, the cars looked like they had been in a war. They were covered in oil, badly painted, and the bodywork looked like it was held together with cheep glue. The engine arrangement had been put together so quickly that bracing tubes were welded over the V8, imprisoning it. The cars behaved badly and were embarrassingly slow. Although Spa was over seven miles long, it was nonetheless a disaster when Hill could only managed to qualify 17th, 12.6 seconds off pole. Baghetti was 20th and last, an amazing 39 seconds off pole! Both cars were to retire in the race with gearbox failure.

When the Dutch Grand Prix rolled around and the team had made some bodywork alterations but when it did not yield any better results, they decided to take a sabbatical from racing to attempt to sort out the car, missing the next two Grand Prix, although Hill did get a drive in France for Ecurie Fillpinetti in a Lotus BRM, eventually not completing enough laps to be classified. ATS had attempted to run the German Grand Prix at the legendary Nurburgring but when their transporter crashed en route to the circuit and since both cars suffered notable damage, they missed that race as well. The team did show up in Monza, the same track where Hill had clinched the World Championship only two years before. At this race, they sported faired hubcaps in an attempt to gain straight-line speed on the fast Italian track. Hill put in a respectable performance to line-up 14th and actually finished the race in 11th, albeit seven laps down. Baghetti actually failed to qualify but after Chris Amon crashed his Lola along with some "convincing" from the race organizers, Isan Raby, Tony Settember, Mario Araujo Cabral, and Carel Godin de Beaufort, all of who were quicker than Baghetti, withdrew their entries. Baghetti started his home Grand Prix. He finished in 15th, 23 laps down.

Many critics expected the struggling effort to skip the final two Grand Prix of the season, as they both took place on the other side of the Atlantic in North America. But make it they did, with Hill being 15th fastest in the 21-car field, 3.7 seconds off pole time. Baghetti was well back of the American and lined-up 20th, only outrunning the Stebro of journeyman Peter Broeker. It was not surprising that both cars were out by the fifth lap and both with oil pump problems. Similarly abysmal results were achieved in the season ending Mexican Grand Prix, with both cars failing to finish once again, Hill out with suspension failure, Baghetti out with another blown engine.

Clearly the team was hopelessly off the pace and short on funds. Thus the ATS team was pulled from the grid after only one season, having only damaged the career of its two talented drivers.

The only other Grand Prix appearance of the ATS 100 came a year later at Monza when Vic Derrington, a supplier of automotive performance equipment, and an Ex-Rob Walker mechanic named Alf Francis modified the now inactive 100 chassis, number 02 to be exact, and as well as using the ATS V8. The entrant was officially a Derrington-Francis/ ATS, so only the ATS engine is credited with the appearance. The car was driven by Mario Araujo Cabral, ironically, one of the men who had been bumped out of the Italian Grand Prix the year before by the Baghetti fiasco. Amazingly, Cabral qualified 19th on the grid, and was involved in a battle with Peter Revson's Lotus/BRM and the BRM of Maurice Trintignant in the race before falling out after 25 laps with ignition problems which silenced his ATS engine. The engine itself was eventually reworked and redressed as a Serenissima (in honor of Count Volpi) and was fitted to the McLaren M2B. It would only compete in three Grand Prix, and its best result came when Bruce McLaren drove it to the sixth place finish in the 1966 British Grand Prix, by far the best result in any Grand Prix for the ATS. It's other two appearances, in Belgium and Holland, resulted in engine problems in practice which in turn resulted in two did not starts. McLaren then reverted back to the Ford Indy engine that he had used in Monaco. The ATS then had its final outing in the back of a customer Cooper T77 ran by Charles Vogele Racing for Swiss driver Silvio Moser at the British Grand Prix of 1967. It retired after 29 laps with, fittingly enough, oil pressure problems.

Another team bearing the ATS named showed up in 1977, but this was named after a German wheel manufacture, Auto Technisches Zubehor.

1969 GOLD LEAF TEAM LOTUS

Chassis: Lotus 63
Engine: Ford Cosworth DFV V8, 3.0-liter normal aspiration
Best Result: 10th (Miles, Great Britain)

IN FORMULA ONE, what is good on paper is not always good on the track. What sounds like an advantage can result in a dismal failure. This is the result for Colin Chapman's dreadful Lotus 63, one of the few true attempts to utilize a four-wheel drive system on a Formula One car.

How do you replace a legend? That is the question Colin Chapman pondered at the end of 1968. His brilliant Lotus 49, now dubbed the 49B after heavy revisions to the aerodynamics, was the class of the field. Graham Hill took the 1968 Championship and things were looking up as the talented Austrian Jochen Rindt was joining the team from the Brabham effort.

But Chapman was not content to sit still. Always on the lookout for new technology, his Lotus 56s had much success in Indy Cars and although part of that was due to its radical Pratt & Whitney turbine engine, the car also used a Ferguson four-wheel drive system. Chapman considered this as a prospect for his Grand Prix machine.

Four-wheel drive was nothing new to auto racing, or to Formula One. In 1902, Spyker built a racecar using the system. In 1961, the Ferguson firm had entered the Claude Hill-designed four-wheel drive P99 in the British Grand Prix with Jack Fairman, and later on Sterling Moss even won the non-Championship outing at Oulton Park in the wet Gold Cup race. But the system was overall not impressive and later a banded. But by the late 1960s, power output and engine torque were growing, and Chapman decided to give the concept another go. In Chapman's theory, the system would allow for better traction off the starting line and accelerating out of the corners by evenly distributing the engines power over four wheels rather than two.

So it was then that Lotus designer Maurice Philippe, under the supervision of Chapman, designed the Lotus 63. The car, four-wheel drive aside, was a development of the 49B and the 56 and 64 Indy Cars. The cars nose bore a strong resemblance to the 49, although the 63 utilized an engine cover with a very flat profile. The rear wing was similar, but not identical, to the 49B, as it had to be mounted in a different fashion. The car was powered by the customary Ford Cosworth DFV, which would soon become standard on virtually all non-factory teams. The DFV was turned back-to-front with the driver sitting just in front of the gearbox. The driver was positioned for forward in the car, with his legs just behind the front suspension. In an effort to make room for the steering an CV joints, the brake discs were inboard, which also reduced unsprung weight. The Firestone rear tires were also replaced with what were effectively front tires, which meant that the car would have less drag and a more even airflow from front to rear.

Despite these innovations, there were problems. For one, the four-wheel drive system was heavy, and added unwanted ballast to the car, which made the drivers complain of "heavy" handling and a problem of finding proper weight distribution from front to rear. There were also problems with the tires, as the rear tires were not up to the task at hand having not been design to operate in those conditions.

It should also be noted that Lotus was not alone in the four-wheel drive adventure. Matra had adapted the system on the MS80, creating the MS84. McLaren had also invested in the concept with the M9A. There was also an unique Robin Herd-designed, Cosworth-built; four-wheel drive machine was also constructed, but withdrawn after testing for the British Grand Prix.

The car's development was short when it made its debut in practice for the Dutch Grand Prix of 1969 in the hands of Graham Hill as Rindt had elected not to drive it, as this was the first serious running the car had. In fact, Rindt had taken a sign that said, "Bargain for sale" from a local Volkswagen dealership and placed it on the 63! Hill struggled in practice, so much so that Hill reverted back to the 49B. With the tried and trusted 49B, Hill lapped the track nearly four seconds faster than he had with the 63, eventually qualifying third behind the Matra of Stewart and Lotus teammate Rindt. Stewart had likewise abandon the MS84 after depressing practice times, going back to the two-wheel drive MS80.

For the next round in France, the 63 was reserved for new Lotus pilot, Englishman John Miles while two factory 49Bs as well as a Rob Walker 49B filled the grid. In qualifying, the 63 was incredibly disappointing, as it lined up 12th in the 13 car field, outpacing only the customer Brabham of Silvio Moser. Miles last only one lap in the race, falling out with fuel pump problems.

In the British Grand Prix a total of four-wheel drive cars filled the grid (which would have been five had the Cosworth shown up). Although Rindt was originally entered in the 63, after practice he refused to drive the car any further and was soon loaned a private 49B from Jo Bonnier as Bonnier was then entrusted with the 63. Add to this the other 63 for John Miles, as well as the Matra of Jean-Pierre Beltoise and the McLaren of Derek Bell. Perhaps no other race epitomized the shortcomings of the system as the four cars filled the final four places of the starting grid. In the race, Bell hit suspension problems after five laps while Bonnier blew an engine only a lap later. Miles finished tenth while running in third gear, while Beltoise finished ninth. There were only ten finishers. The McLaren would never run again.

For the German Grand Prix, it was Mario Andretti, the impressive Italian-American, who would shoulder the responsibility of the 63. Mario lined up the 12th fastest of the 14 cars but lost control on the first lap and totally destroyed the 63.

Although Rindt had avoided the 63 after the dismal Silverstone showing, Chapman out his foot down and entered Rindt in the International Gold Cup non-Championship race at Oulton Park. Thus, the only time that Rindt would actually compete in the 63, it produced the cars best result, a second. Although second was a fine result for the car, it was a lap behind Jackie Ickx in a less than a spectacular field which included Hill competing in an F2 Lotus as there was only one 63 left after the Andretti accident.

Improvements to the car were made, but they did little good. The team moved more of the power output to the rear of the car and some aerodynamic modifications such as a smaller rear wing and an altered nose.

Miles drove the car in three more Grand Prix, failing to finish each time. Andretti had one more start in the car, that coming at his home Grand Prix in Watkins Glen, New York, only to suffer suspension failure after only three laps.

The 63 was deemed a failure and the team would have to wait until early 1970 before a permanent replacement was found for the 49B, that being the radical 72. Chapman again tried the system briefly in 1971 on his Indy-derived Lotus 56B with a turbine engine, but in fact kept the front-wheel drive 72 through 1975! Other constructors such as March and later Williams toyed with the idea before four-wheel drive was banned outright in 1983.

As a final, tragic note, John Dawson-Damer was tragically killed in one of the remaining 63s when his car went off in the 2000 edition of the Goodwood Festival of Speed.

1971 GOLD LEAF TEAM LOTUS

(WORLD WIDE RACING)

Chassis: Lotus 56B
Engine: Pratt & Whitney turbine
Best Result: 8th (Fittipaldi, Italy)

TEAM LOTUS BOSS Colin Chapman was always willing to take risks. Sometimes it worked, sometimes it didn't. One of the times it didn't came in 1971 when Chapman attempted to run a gas turbine powered car. It was a project with vast potential but was perhaps too large a developmental process for it to succeed.

The year is 1967. Parnelli Jones, driving for Andy Granatelli's STP squad, dominates the Indy 500 using a unique Pratt & Whitney ST6B-62 gas turbine engine, producing 550 horsepower, only to fall out of the race on lap 196 when a $5 bearing in the gear casing failed. It allowed A.J. Foyt to win the race, but the real story was the turbine of Jones. The engine had upstaged the long established Offenhauser engine as well as the Ford, and now everyone couldn't stop talking about it.

What is a gas turbine? A gas turbine engine produces pressurized gas by burning gasoline. The heat that builds up from this process expands the air, which in turn spins the turbine. Turbines have had many uses over the years, powering everything from commercial jets to helicopters and even tanks.

The STP effort of 1967 was a breakthrough. Everyone realized this, including Team Lotus boss Colin Chapman. Chapman had won the

Indy 500 with Jim Clark with Ford Power in 1965 and have had STP connections as they had also sponsored his cars at Indy. So Chapman, never one afraid to take a risk, would field a fleet of gas turbine Lotus entries for the 1968 Indy 500 in conjunction with Granatelli and STP despite USAC regulations requiring that the inlet area for the turbine be restricted, which lowered the power output of the turbine to approximately 450 horsepower.

The cars would be dubbed the Lotus 56, and like Granatelli the year before, would also receive turbine engines from Pratt & Whitney, a leading producer of marine and aerospace turbine engines. The engines supplied to the Indy effort were the ST6B-70 variation.

Jim Clark was to be one of the drivers for this effort in car number 30, but fate would deal a crushing blow when he was killed in Germany in the spring of 1968 in a Formula 2 race. Mike Spence, another Grand Prix driver, replaced Clark but he too lost his life in the Lotus during practice for the race. But on pole day, Joe Leonard took the pole position while Lotus Grand Prix regular Graham Hill took second. A third Lotus Pratt & Whitney was originally intended for Jackie Stewart but the Scotsman had suffered a broken wrist while racing in Europe, so he was replaced by Art Pollard, who lined up in the middle of row four in the 11th starting position.

The race was a disappointment. None of the turbines would finish 500 miles. Hill crashed on his 124th lap while Leonard ran at the front all day and was actually leading with ten laps remaining when his fuel pump shaft failed while under a yellow flag. Pollard suffered an identical failure at virtually the same time. Granatelli had questioned the fuel pump shafts before the race, and he was to be proven correct.

Questions were raised as to how the car would perform on a road course. Those questions were given some answers when Chapman ran the 56 on the road courses of USAC later in the year. On average, the turbines ran surprisingly well.

In 1969, the Lotus team again entered the Indy 500 but faced even stricter inlet rules put forth by USAC and settled for Ford power. These rule changes would render the turbine virtually uncompetitive at Indianapolis (before being banned outright in 1970). The Lotus Indy efforts for 1969 was fruitless anyway as Chapman had withdrawn the team after a manufacturing error with the hub carriers was found after a practice crash involving Mario Andretti. But Chapman was not quite done with the turbine concept. Chapman had plans to put together a Formula One Car that would be powered by the Pratt & Whitney turbine engines.

Chapman had been instrumental in convincing Ford to finance the Cosworth DFV (or, double four-valve), an engine that Lotus had dominated Formula One with, as only reliability cost Clark the 1967 title and Hill won the Championship outright in 1968. But now, the Cosworth was available to most teams, and Chapman had hoped to have a similar impact with the turbine.

Chapman had actually planned to take the 56 into Grand Prix Racing earlier, but the 3.0-liter equivalent formula wasn't yet available. The formula was a complex system that utilized Capacity of the regular engine runner, times 0.09625, divided by the product of 3.10 times Ratio of the turbine minus 7.63. The car tested during 1970, where it was discovered that it had throttle lag and braking problems. The hope was to run the car in Monza that year, but it didn't. In fact, it was a race that Lotus would love to forget, as Jochen Rindt, the leader drive for Lotus, crashed heavily in practice when attempting to drive with no rear wing, which resulted in the withdraw of all Lotus entries. Rindt would be fatally injured but had scored enough points to become the first and only posthumous World Champion.

Finally, the 56B would appear in official competition in 1971, although for most of the year the team would still run the 1970 Championship winning Lotus 72, now being dubbed the Lotus "72D" as new suspension and aero pieces carried the groundbreaking car into its second season. The 56B was a modified 56 frame that featured very svelte bugles on the sides in order to bring fuel loads up to that required for a Grand Prix distance. In addition, it featured a large two element rear wing that somewhat resembled the wing on the Lotus 72. Two front wings were also added to the machine. It also featured large square braking ducts on both sides of the car just behind the driver. The Lotus 56B made use of a Ferguson full time four-wheel drive system. Chapman had previously tried four-wheel drive on the disappointing Lotus 63 (which both works drivers Hill and Rindt hated with a passion), as had other constructors such as Matra and McLaren, but the system was handicapped because it required teams to run what were in effect four front tire, for which the Lotus team was supplied by Firestone. The 56B would make use of Pratt & Whitney's STN76 engine, which had previously seen life as a Military Helicopter power plant, and was built at the company's facility in Longueil, Quebec. The power output was reputed to be around 500 horsepower, which was a modest gain over the Cosworth runners. The car had only one forward gear for the drivers to make use of.

The 56B had many shortcomings. For one, it was heavy. Although turbines have good power-to-weight ratio, the car had to carry a lot of fuel, 350 liters worth in fact. The wedge-shaped 56B had many aerodynamic problems because of the compromises of the turbine, and it was soon obvious that the engine, which needed to have time to spin before being useful, had terrible throttle response in addition to no engine braking which also put extra ware on the brakes. That meant that the driver would have to drastically change his braking and acceleration points when entering and exiting corners. This problem was unforeseen in Indianapolis because the driver is on the throttle for most of the time. In addition, the Ferguson four-wheel drive system, which was put in to try and reduce the massive torque from the engine, was heavy, which added yet more weight to the already large machine. Also, the fact that it was a three-year-old design didn't help matters.

The car made its debut at the non-Championship race of Champions at Brands Hatch. Emerson Fittipaldi would drive the machine. Fittipaldi put it on the front row but suffered from the car bottoming for much of his race before finally the rear suspension had enough and the car was out. Rear suspension failures were not surprising considering that Lotus had a reputation for making extremely light and nimble cars. In fact, suspension failures were the main reason for the 56B failing to finish its first three events, which were all non-Championship races. Dave Walker, who was the Lotus test driver, looked as if he would be competitive at the combined F1/F5000 race in Hockenheim, as the turbine would be well suited to the long straights on the German circuit. However, the 56B suffered an uncommon engine failure during practice and since there was no spare, the team's weekend was finished.

The first Championship appearance of the turbine would come at the Dutch Grand Prix; with Walker again getting the driving duties while Reine Wisell was entered in the trusted Lotus 72. Fittipaldi had a road accident in France leading up to the race, and South African Dave Charlton was put in to replace him. However, Charlton crashed on Friday and the car would not race. In qualifying, it was no contest between the 72 and the 56B. Wisell lined up sixth on the grid, only 1.2 seconds off Jacky Ickx's pole time. Walker could only manage the 22nd fastest time however, full 4.4 seconds away from the pole winning Ferrari and 3.2 seconds off the Lotus 72. But in the race, wet weather played into the hands of Walker and the 56B. Walker climbed up to as high as tenth as was lapping faster than Ickx, an acknowledged rain master, when he misjudged his braking distance going into the Tarzan corner and spun off on the fifth lap. Chapman's disgust was evident; as this was the best the car had performed since its inception. It is debatable whether the car benefited from its turbine engine or its four-wheel drive, but this is the closet the car would come to looking competitive.

The next appearance for the car came at Silverstone with Wisell behind the wheel while Fittipaldi and Charlton were both entered in Lotus 72s. Back in those days, Silverstone was a track with long straights and long, sweeping corners, which one would think would suite the turbine well. Fittipaldi put his 72 fourth on the starting line while Charlton was back in 13th. Wisell was much slower however, and could only manage the 19th fastest time. Wisell completed 57 laps but was not classified.

The final Championship appearance for the 56B came at Monza, Italy, the same track where Rindt had been killed a year earlier driving the wingless lotus 72. Due to continuing legal problems from the Rindt accident, the Lotus team would enter under the name "World

Wide Racing", which replaced "Gold Leaf Team Lotus". Fittipaldi would be the sole Lotus driver for this event and the red, white, and gold colors of Gold Leaf were replaced by a bizarre gold and black machine. Monza is one of the fastest tracks in the world, with few corners and long straights, but high temperatures meant that the turbine couldn't must its full power and Fittipaldi, the lead Lotus driver, could only muster 18th on the grid but he did manage to finish the race in eighth position, a lap behind. Fittipaldi is convinced that the car he drove in Monza was actually the car that Mike Spence had lost his life in back in 1968. The final time the 56B raced was one week later in Hockenheim in the Rothmans 5000 Championship race, again with Fittipaldi. The Brazillian, who was to become World Champion a season later, brought the car home a fine second. Emerson later said it was the worst car he had ever driven.

The 56B was really only intended as a test vehicle with a more advanced machine planned for 1972 possibly using only two-wheel drive, but for numerous reasons the project was cancelled. For one, Lotus had endured a horrible season, scoring only 21 points and failing to win a race. Also, to race you must please your sponsors, and to please your sponsors, you must produce results. And speaking of money, a lot of it had been waited on the concept. Add to that, Pratt & Whitney were beginning to lose interest in the project, as most of their glory had come back in 1967 and 1968. Chapman also blamed the failure of the car on the heavy four-wheel drive system, which some people think actually was the best part of the project.

Had the 56B worker or even showed some serious potential, perhaps Chapman would have revolutionized the sport the same way he did with ground effect technology some years later. But in Formula One, new concepts are either dominate and picked up on by everyone else or tossed to the side forever locked in the lines of time. For the 56B the result was the later.

1972 TEAM EIFELLAND CARAVANS

Chassis: March 721
Engine: Ford Cosworth DFV V8, 3.0-liter normal aspiration
Best Result: 10th (Stommelen, Monaco & Great Britain)

WHEN THE MARCH team entered Formula One in 1970, it was first as a factory. But when they failed to lure away top drivers such as Jochen Rindt for their own outfit, they jumped at the chance of signing Ken Tyrrell's team and reigning champion Jackie Stewart to a contract for the 1970 season. During the rest of the 1970s, March would supply such teams as Penske and Williams, but the oddest team to ever use a March chassis was the Eifelland team in 1972.

Gunter Henerici, owner of the Caravan Company Eifelland Wohnwagenbau, headed the Eifelland team. Henerici had been a sponsor of German driver Rolf Stommelen since his Formula 2 days that eventually led to drivers in Formula One with Brabham and the Surtees, with a highlight being a third in Austria in 1970. It would be no surprise that when Henerici proposed to Stommelen that they from their own effort, the young German would agree.

The new team would use a customer March chassis. The March team had raced in Formula One since 1970 and its founding members Max Mosley, Alan Rees, Graham Coaker, and Robin Herd, were keen to see the project succeed. Jackie Stewart had given the team a startling victory in its first year under the Tyrell Racing banner, and Ronnie Peterson had finished a strong second to Stewart in the 1971 Championship using the STP sponsored factory March 711 with its infamous "tea tray" front wing. The Swedish driver didn't record a victory, but he did finish second four times.

The 1972 machine was to be even better. The "721X" would feature the gearbox mounted between the engine and the axle in efforts to improve handling. The team's hopes were based on this radical machine, so it was discouraging when Niki Lauda told the team it was a failure early its development. After both Niki and Peterson both failed to achieve results, and an F2 based replacement known as the 721G("G" standing for Guinness Book of Records for the record time of nine days that it took to put together) was hurriedly produced. The customer teams would make use of the standard 721, the customers being Frank Williams the Eifelland for Stommelen.

But this would be no ordinary March that Srommelen would step into. The designer of this machine would be a Swedish man known as Luigi Colani. This man was seemingly obsessed with curves and the roundness of objects. Colani had started out as a designer for Fiat and had produced the 1957 Colani Alfa sportscar. He then went on to design the 1959 BMW 700 monocoque sportscar. Two of his more famous creations include the Canon T90 photocamera and the Mazda MX5 sportscar. Moving on to work in the aircraft and furniture industry and even designing the Colani Highscreen PC. Despite his impressive resume, however, Colani had virtually no single-seater experince to speak of before joining Eifelland.

Colani would rework the customer 721 to the point where it didn't resemble the original March at all. The airbox was moved from the top of the roll hoop to just in front of the driver, and the standard double rear view mirrors were gone in favor of a bizarre periscope-style mirror that would be fitted in the middle of the single piece cockpit, making Stommelen look up to see what was behind him. The car also featured an unusual one-piece rear wing in addition to a strange nose that looked like it came from the pages of science fiction rather that engineering. Like most every other team of the era, Eifelland would use the superb Ford Cosworth DFV, which set the standards in Formula One engineering.

From the beginning, there were problems. The original nose that

Colani designed was prone to overheating and the car missed the season opener in Argentina and then showed up in South Africa using the "tea tray" from the March factory, which would eventually give way to the new 721 nose. Stommelen did a respectable job to get the radical machine onto the grid in 25th position, which was encouraging considering he was only 1.5 seconds off the pace of Lauda's works March. The German the finished the race, albeit in 13th position and two laps behind Denny Hulme's race winning McLaren.

Before the next race in Jarama, Spain, the team made alterations to the car, which included sidepods that resembled those found on the factory machines, as well as a new blue and white livery. There was also a chronic lack of downface which made the car difficult to drive, eventually leading the one piece rear wing being replaced by a more conventional two piece element.

Perhaps this is why that Stommelen was able to qualify 17th on the grid, ahead of the Williams March of Henri Pescarolo and the works March 721X of Lauda, who just made it onto the grid in 25th position. Mike Beuttler, in another customer March 721G, failed to qualify. In the race, Stommelen lasted only 15 laps before spinning off, but the performance had given the team signs of hope.

The next round came in Monaco, and it was one of Eifelland's best result. The weekend didn't get off to the best possible start as Stommelen found a lack of grip on the tight and twisty circuit to be troublesome and was by far the slowest car in qualifications. He was 8.1 seconds off the pole time of Emerson Fittipaldi's Lotus and was nearly three seconds slower than the next slowest runner, Carlos Pace, in the Williams March 711.

The race was ran in monsoon conditions and while everyone was taken back by the vixtory of Jean Pierre Beltoise (which was the final victory for BRM), the rainy weather allowed Stommelen to finish tenth, even beating the ultra quick Peterson in the factory car.

The next race was in Nivelles, Belgium. The Nivelles track had replaced the much-loved Spa circuit after Spa was reported to be too fast and too long. Stommelen could only 20th on the grid, but he did not qualify Lauda in the dissappoingting factory 721X and Mike

Beuttler in the Clarke-Mordaunt-Guthrie Racing customer March 72G. On raceday, Stommelen finished 11th and beat the 72X of Lauda and was actually on the same lap as Peterson who finished ninth. The real March star of the day was Carlos Pace in the Williams March, as he had finished a fine fifth.

In France, Stommelen would qualify 15th, actually posting an identical time of 2'59.6 around the Clermont Ferrand Circuit with the Tyrrell Ford of Patrick Depailler. He was still ahead of Lauda but Peterson, finally coming to terms with the new 721G, qualified a brilliant ninth with Pace's Williams March two spots back in 11th. Despite a pitstop to replace a punctured tire, Stommelen finished a lap down in 16th place.

On to the British Grand Prix, which was held at Brands Hatch in 1972. Stommelen was the slowest of the March runners after Lauda had gotten into his works 721G and the German could only line up 25th fastest. In a race of attrition, Stommelen finished tenth, one spot and two laps behind the works effort of Lauda.

At the legendary Nurburing, Stommelen put in an excellent drive on the monster track to qualify 14th, again out running Lauda but Peterson came into his own by driving the reluctant 721G to an amazing fourth on the grid. Although Peterson would eventually finish third, Stommelen was out after only six laps due to electrical problems.

By this time however, there was trouble on the horizon. Henerici had sold his Caravan business to a party, which had no interest in auto racing, and in particular spending money on auto racing. Thus, money quickly became a problem.

In what would turn out to be the final race for the car, the entry was under the "Team Stommelen" name in Austria. The skeleton crew prepared the car good enough for Rolf to qualify 17th, but after pitstops to repair the bodywork, Stommelen's race ended on lap 48 when his Cosworth experienced a rare engine failure.

Out of money, the team was a no-show for the final three Grand Prix of the season. There were some Eifelland Formula 3 cars, called Type 23, competing which were based on the March 723, although this project would also meet its end just as the Grand Prix team had. The internal structure of the team eventually became known as Hexagon Racing, and would compete at a number of non-Championship events.

The failure of Eifelland could be described as a failure of a dream. The dream to design a futuristic and fun shaped F1 car and to make it successful. However, that dream turned into a nightmare when one discovers that usually, the more boring and bland you make your car, generally, the more reliable and successful it will be.

1974 CHRIS AMON RACING

Chassis: Amon AF1
Engine: Ford Cosworth DFV V8, 3.0-liter normal aspiration
Best Result: DNF (Amon, Spain)

CHRIS AMON HAS been called the best Formula One driver never to win a Grand Prix. The record book would back up that claim, as he won five pole positions, set three fastest laps, and finished on the podium three times despite coming up short in the win column (although he did win several non-Championship F1 races as well as the 24 Hours of Le Mans). In his later Grand Prix years, Chris was handed some truly lackluster equipment, one of which bared his own name, the Amon Af1.

Chris Amon's career had been somewhat derailed by the time that 1974 had arrived. Once seen as an aspiring young racer, Chris had been wasting his time in 1973 with the disappointing Techno team, an effort where his talent far exceeded the car underneath him. After two guests drivers in the season ending Canadian and United States Grand Prixs (of which the later was withdrawn following a fatal accident involving teammate Francois Cevert), he was again on the way out for 1974.

That is when he decided to do Formula One his own way, with his own team. Owner/drivers are rare in Formula One, and successful owner/drivers are even rarer, as the only ones to have managed to make this work include Jack Brabham, the late Bruce McLaren, and Dan Gurney.

But this actually wasn't the first team he had his own team, as he had attempted (and failed) to enter a private Brabham in the 1966 Italian Grand Prix. But now, it was to be a full effort. His funding would come from a man named John Dalton. Designing the machine would be the creative Gordon Fowell, the same man who Amon had commissioned to design the disappointing Techno the previous season. The car, dubbed the AF1, was built in John Thompson's garage.

The car featured several innovative features, such as the single fuel tank mounted between the driver and engine, a forward position for the driver, and titanium torsion bar suspension had replaced the usual coil spring system. The AF1 also featured inboard brakes. The engine of choice was, like every other non-Ferrari or BRM runner, was powered by the Ford Cosworth V8, which in Amon's case, maintained by with Ray Buckley. Like many other teams, the Amon made use of a Hewland gearbox. The powder blue car also featured an unusually mounted front wing, which was actually on the nose rather than below it. The nose itself was reversed and curved, to battle aerodynamic lift. The car used Firestone tires rather than readily available Goodyear's.

The AF1 was originally intended to run the full season, starting in Brazil, but when testing yielded numerous problems, the debut was set back. One of the frequent problems involved the wheels leaving the car while at speed, which if you can't guess, is not great for the driver confidence. Another problem with the car was it's structural strength, or lack of. To improve this, the team had to make the car stronger and in turn heavier, and whenever one makes a car heavier, it is slower and harder to drive.

The debut finally came in the Spanish Grand Prix at the Jarma Circuit. The car, now sporting a traditional front wing, qualified 24th on the starting grid. This eventually became 23rd when the March of Vittorio Brambilla didn't make the starting grid. Despite vibrations in qualifying, Amon bravely lined up on the grid. Starting the race on wet tires, Amon lasted a cautious 22 laps before becoming the fourth retirement because of a brake shaft failure. Little did he know it at the time, but it would be the only time he would actually race the Af1.

Further testing problems meant the team would not take part in the following round in Belgium.

In the Monaco, the Amon team can ready with a new front wing, which resemabled the front wing found on the March and the previous year's Tyrrell. The brakes were back to outboard and used a front radiator. Chris did an admirable job to take the sluggish machine into 20th qualifying position. He would not start the race, however, as a wheel hub failure prevented him from making the staring line up.

Yet more problems meant that the Amon effort would be absent from the French and British races before the team showed up at the Nurburgring. Amon was in the car briefly on the monster circuit before falling ill and handing the car over to Australian Larry Perkins. Not surprisingly, Perkins was unable to bring the car up to speed and was the slowest car in qualifying, over 45 seconds off Niki Lauda's pole time, and entering non –qualification.

The Amon team missed Austria but attempted to qualify for the Italian Grand Prix at Monza, Amon had nearly won at Monza two years earlier, but had been robbed of his (and Matra's) first Formula One victory when his visor came away from his helmet, causing him to slow. Perhaps this best demonstrated the shortcomings of the chassis, and despite the fact that the team was again using side mounted radiators, Amon failed to qualify and was over five seconds off pole time. Aside from the AAW Surtees of Finnish rookie Leo Kinnunen, the Amon was the slowest car in the field.

The Amon project had certainly disappointed, and it was not surprising to see the team fold after the terrible weekend at Monza as they were short on sponsors and out of money. Amon would get a couple of guests drivers in the virtually sponsorless BRM team at the end of 1974 before spending two seasons at Morris Nunn's English team. A final drive in the disappointing Wolf-Williams in Canada resulted in a grid position, only to be taken away by an accident during the second qualifying session. Amon never got the Grand Prix victory that he wanted, and rightly deserved, so badly, and the Amon AF1 effort (which saw Chris turn down a drive with Brabham to operate) only added to the New Zelander's frustrations.

1979 TEAM REBAQUE

Chassis: Rebaque HR100
Engine: Ford Cosworth DFV V8, 3.0-liter normal aspiration
Best Result: DNF (Rebaque, Canada)

BACK IN THE old days, the term "Privateer" was a common one. Rather than build ones own chassis, a team would buy their chassis from another constructor. The most famous of these would probably be Rob Walker, who was highly successful in the art with customer Coopers and Lotuses. Perhaps the last honest attempt to make this process work came from Hector Rebaque, who bought year old Lotuses in the late 1970s. But what many people forget is that Hector actually raced his own car towards the end of 1979, and while the car might have been pleasing to the eye, it was less than a success and quickly faded into the background.

Hector Rebaque has been called the last of the Gentleman drivers. He grew up in a wealthy family and his father, Hector Alonso Rebaque, was an accomplished architect who had a hand in developing new portions of Mexico City. Rebaque came to Europe at the age of 18 to pursue a single seater career and soon he was competing in Formula 2. After two years back in the Canadian Atlantic series, Hector made the huge leap into Formula One.

Hector jointed the Hesketh team and made his debut at Spa in the team's 308E chassis as a teammate to Harald Ertl. It was certainly not an instant success, as Hector failed to qualify in his first three attempts. He did make on the grid in Germany only to succumb to a Cosworth engine failure while his last two starts yielded two more DNQs.

Hector had limited options heading into 1978 so he decided to setup his own family owned operation in which he would not only be the driver but also team principal as well. The team set up base in Lemington, Spa and Ian Dawson was the general manager. But Rebaque would not build his own chassis as he had came to terms with Team Lotus boss Colin Chapman to use year old Lotus 78s. The Lotus 78 had won five races the previous season and was ground breaking in that it featured ground effect technology, which was still in its infancy. It was thought that this would produce at least mid-field results, but it was a struggle in the beginning failing to qualify several times and collecting only one point after a sixth place in Germany.

For 1979 things looked better. Hector would again use a year old Lotus, but now he would have the incredible Lotus 79 that Mario Andretti had dominated the 1978 season with. The 79 was the first car to truly capture ground effect technology by using wing shaped tunnels under the car to generate tremendous road holding. Rebaque once again struggled but usually qualified. Not that it affected Rebaque, but the car Lotus had intended to replace the 79 with, the Lotus 80, was a failure and Lotus resorted back to using the 79 as well for the most of the season.

Seeing that he could not continue with the 79 forever and also frustrated with the lack of support from the Lotus factory, Rebaque began plans to build his own chassis. The HR100 was to run at end of the 1979 season and plans were to take the entry into 1980.

The HR 100 actually had a high pedigree. It was commissioned to Penske Racing and designed at the Penske base in Pool, England under the hand of design expert Geoff Ferris but then reworked by John Barnard, who is in just a few seasons would design the all-conquering line of McLaren MP4s. The engine of choice was the traditional Ford Cosworth DFV, which was available to virtually any team that wanted one. The car was fitted with Goodyear tires, just as the customer Lotus had been. It has been suggested that the HR100 was nothing more than a Lotus 79 with a few extra parts. Speculation has it that the running gear and the suspension of the Lotus 79 were bolted to the new chassis. The HR100 did look similar to the 79, but it was not identical. It had a different side pod arrangement including tall fins in front of the rear tires. In fact, this part of the car resembled the Williams more than it did the Lotus. Did it borrow heavily from the 79? Absolutely, but not many cars from 1979 didn't try and copy the ground breaking machine. Sponsorship on the brown and gold car was minimal, but did have some support from Marlboro of Mexico and the Carta Blanca beer brand.

The HR100 was completed in time to enter the final three races of the season. At Monza, Rebaque could only muster the 28th fastest time and failed to qualify on the fast Italian circuit. Then in Canada, Hector snuck on the grid by posting the 22nd fastest time. In the race, Hector completed 26 laps before suffering an unusual failure with the engine mounting. In the season ending United States Grand Prix at Watkins Glen, Rebaque was 28th fastest, only out qualifying Alex Ribero's Fittipaldi and Arturo Merzario's Merzario. Two DNQ's in three starts didn't spell success and the proposed HR 101 for 1980 never came to life after the Rebaque team was denied entry into the Formula One Constructors Association (FOCA).

Thus the Rebaque saga ends here. Deals were made and broken, promises were forgotten, and for Hector the burden of managing a Grand Prix team while also driving was too much. The Mexican didn't start the 1980 season but got a huge break when Brabham fired Ricardo Zunino after a disappointing start to the season. The team then asked Hector, who came with some sponsorship, to take the second seat. While he was a firm number two to Nelson Piquet, he did have the occasional good performance (scoring a trio of fourth place finishes) before being replaced at the end of 1981 by Ricardo Patrese. After a short career in Indy Car racing, which included one victory, Hector retired from major auto racing following an accident at Michigan Speedway.

Stricter rules from the governing body eventually saw the demise of racers such as Rebaque simply buying old factory machines and racing them, forcing the teams to construct their own machinery. This meant we would never again see combinations like Walker-Coopers, Tyrrell-Matras, and yes, Rebaque-Lotuses. And while Formual One may have became a neater and more organized sport, perhaps it also lost a link to a part of its history as well.

ESSEX TEAM LOTUS/JOHN PLAYER

SPECIAL TEAM LOTUS

Chassis: Lotus 88/88B
Engine: Ford Cosworth DFV V8, 3.0-liter normal-aspiration
Best Result: Disqualified

EVERY TEAM IN Formula One has the intentions to push, and sometimes break, the rules of the governing body. Perhaps no example of this is better illustrated than the infamous "double chassis" Lotus 88 and then 88B of Colin Chapman. We will never know what the car could have achieved, because it was banned before it ever took part in a Grand Prix.

Colin Chapman had always been a daring, innovative designer. He showed that with the Lotus 43, 49, 72 and 79 designs which broke the mold of a Formula One car's construction. His latest work of the, the 79, was truly a world beater, winning both the drivers and constructors titles with Mario Andretti and Ronnie Peterson behind the wheel. It used wing shaped sidepods to generate huge amounts of downforce from the underbody of the car, which was sealed by sliding skirts. Cornering speed was increased dramatically, but the driver's comfort was sacrificed due to the concept requiring an incredibly stiff suspension to be effective.

The year is now 1980. After the dream that had been 1978, 1979 had been a nightmare. Chapman had seen his daring Lotus 80 become a failure. The car was an awesome looking piece, originally with only a low-lying rear wing and an incredible underbody, which was virtually, all wing shaped. Although wind tunnel tests were promising, Mario Andretti drove it in only three Grand Prixs and although the American managed a podium in France, the team soon returned to the year-old 79 with less that spectacular results.

Now the team was stuck on mediocrity with their Lotus 81, which was not up to par with the Williams and Brabham teams. Chapman knew he had to try something radical to regain his position, and his idea was nothing short of amazing. A double chassis Formula One car.

The theory behind the double chassis concept was to basically mount a second body onto the tub of the car to get around the new ban on sliding skirts FISA had introduced for 1981. The first chassis consisted of the basic aluminum honeycomb monocoque, with its suspension layout (which included generally soft springs), fuel tank, drivetrain, and engine. The second chassis included the separately mounted bodywork of the car, sidepods, radiators, and wings. It was mounted by stiff springs onto the suspension uprights. This allowed the car to generate ground effect without using the hard shock and spring package, which had become virtually mandatory to suck the car to the road but had literally beaten up its pilots. The car's down-force would also be generated directly onto the tire. In a sense, it would be easier on the car and the driver while a more effective way of producing grip. Like virtually every other British team, power came from Ford's impeccable Cosworth DFV while an F1 pull out from Goodyear meant that the Lotus 88 would run on Michelins. In time, Goodyear would return to the sport and the 88.

The double chassis concept was introduced as a test vehicle in 1980 with the Lotus 86, which was based on the 81. At the time, it was suspected that the team might face legal problems with the car and a separate car was built, the Lotus 87 which was also based on the 81 chassis.

Despite some resistance, the 88 went ahead for the season open-ing United States Grand Prix at Long beach. It passed inspection, and the car practiced with Elio de Angelis behind the wheel. On Friday the car failed with fuel pressure problems early on and Elio reverted back to the 81. Afterward a record 11 protests were filed claiming the car was illegal. Early Saturday de Angelis was lapping the track in the 1.22 region after complaining of balance problems. He completed only 14 laps before being black-flagged off the course. The Lotus team then reverted back to the old 81for qualifying and the race. This despite the American FIA having held a hearing and eventually finding the car legal.

A similar situation occurred in Rio, Brazil. The Lotus team had conducted a testing session on the Wednesday leading up the Grand Prix with de Angelis working on an understeer problem. He recorded the fifth quickest time, which was approximately two seconds slower than the Williams of Carlos Reutemann. The car passed inspection but was banned from competition after the 88 completed only two laps. It didn't get past inspection in Argentina, at which Chapman took out his frustrations in an outspoken press conference where he claimed that the Formula One Championship had degenerated into a power struggle between "money men". This resulted in a steep $100,000 fine from FISA for placing the integrity of the championship in doubt. Chapman left the team and flew back to England, which was something out of character for the Englishman.

An appeal was heard before the FIA in Paris France, but despite the best efforts of Chapman, the ruling stood. As a protest, Chapman boycotted the San Marino Grand Prix before debuting the new 87 in Monaco.

After all the dust cleared, the Lotus team continued with the 87 for the next two races in Spain and France, in which de Angelis managed fifth and sixth place finishes while the second car of Nigel Mansell took sixth and seventh. A change of livery was included, as the team had changed from Essex livery back to the legendary black and gold John Player Special cigarette colors that Lotus had ran from 1972 to 1978.

Then came Chapman's home Grand Prix of Silverstone. Lotus had conducted tests with both the 88B and the 87 in testing before the Grand Prix with Mansell as well as test driver Roberto Moreno. The team showed up with three double chassis machines, the 88 and two-88Bs. The 88Bs were 88s with altered bodywork and relocated oil cooler. Somewhat surprisingly, the cars passed RAC inspection and were almost immediately protested by the "factory" teams of Ligier, Alfa Romeo, and Ferrari. The 88Bs were allowed to practice while the hearing went on regarding the legality of the cars. FISA disagreed with the legality of the cars and threatened to declare the 1981 British Grand Prix non-Championship. The stewards gave into the demands of FISA and Lotus then had to convert their 88B back to 87 spec. A look at the times does not reveal that the car would have been dominate, as de Angelis managed a 1.16.029 in the 88B while qualifying with a 1.15.971 in the 87. Mansell did little better and actually failed to qualify in the 87. Despite the results, there was skepticism, just as there had been at Long Beach, that the Lotus drivers were holding back, not wanting to reveal performance of the machine.

The Lotus 88 was now confined to the history books. Lotus spent the rest of the year developing the 87 with Mansell's third in Belgium being the best result as the 88's development had taken much on the team's budget. The teams efforts were put into 1982 when Chapman would see victory only once more in his career, that coming when de Angelis edged Keke Rosberg in Austria. Team moral at Lotus was crushed when Chapman died of a heart attack in December of that year, at the height of legal problems stemming from his involvement in the John DeLorean supercar fiasco.

The Lotus 88 remains one of the biggest "what ifs" in the history of Formula One. Although legally correct, many felt the 88 broke the sprit of the rules while at the same time, many team principles feared that the concept would make their challengers obsolete.

1986 MOTOR RACING DEVELOPMENTS LTD.

(BRABHAM BMW)

Chassis: Brabham BT55
Engine: BMW in-line 4, 1.5 liter turbo charged
Best Result: 6th (Patrese, San Marino & USA-Detroit)

THE 1986 "SKATEBOARD" Brabham was a truly radical, complex, and above all tragic Formula One car. Its sharp lines and bold blue and white colors hiding its many deficiencies. The concept was intriguing, but not viable.

The Brabham name is one that is normally thought of when one thinks of winning cars. Jack Brabham was the only person ever to win the World Championship with a car of his own construction in 1966. When Bernie Ecclestone purchased the team in the early 1970s, he had every intent of keeping the tradition alive. And he did. After hiring designer Gordon Murry along with Pete Weismann, the Brabham team won the 1981 Drivers title with Brazilian Nelson Piquet in the BT49, and again in 1983 with Piquet using the BMW powered BT52, which marked the first title for a turbo-charged engine. The team was known for its radical innovations in ground effect technology and also reintroducing re-fueling to Formula One. But during 1984, the BMW in-line 4 turbo experienced numerous reliability woes and other teams were beginning to catch up with Murry's designs. A switch form Michelin to Pirelli tires for 1985 didn't help, with Piquet taking only a win in France for his troubles. The Brabham team had a strong relationship with BMW, with the tiny 1.5-liter in-line 4-cylinder engine making a rumored

1400 horsepower. But even though they had a power advantage, it did not put the team back on top.

That is why in the middle if the 1985 season Murry, unhappy with the aerodynamic shortcomings of the BT54, proposed a radical concept for his next car. A "low lone" car that would be packaged incredibly small and nimble where the driver would be seated at a laid back position. The idea was given to him in part by Piquet, who recalled laying his head down in his Formula 3 days while trying to achieve maximum aerodynamic benefit. A wooden model of the car was presented to Piquet who reportedly wasn't thrilled about the driving position. Piquet would not have to worry about it though, as by August of 1985 it was known that he would move to Williams in 1986.

Enter the BT55. The car would have many things that would distinguish it from the rest of the grid. For one, it would be the first time in modern Grand Prix racing that an engine and a gearbox were tilted at an 18-degree angle into the chassis and moved over to the right of the car, in part to improve the center of gravity but also a necessity if they were to fit in the car. It also had a unique 7-speed gearbox, a first in Formula One, because the standard Hewland could not be adapted to the offset crankshaft. For BMW's Paul Rosche, this was more than a case of just putting in the systems differently, as his BMW turbos were modified to great lengths to appease the design and Brabham's engines would differ from the standard issues received by Benetton and Arrows, although they would eventually behave quite similar. The BT55 would also feature the longest wheelbase in the pit lane, which is also somewhat because of the engine and bevel-drive transmission configuration.

The nose of the car was also unique in that the rear view mirrors were incorporated into the design instead of just being placed on later in the design process. Murry had hoped for a 10% savings in the frontal area of the machine. All in all, the BT55 was some 28 centimeters lower that the previous BT54. The cockpit was so small that only four-point seat belts could be use, rather than the standard six-point. Because of the laid-back driver position, it was also hoped that additional air would move to the rear of the car generating more down force (as much as 30% more than the BT54) with a smaller rear wing, as only a smaller roll bar interrupted the airflow. Murry had been one of the leaders in using push-rod suspension, but in keeping with the low center of gravity theme, the BT55 featured pull-rod.

The driver line-up for this machine remained a mystery for some time, however. Ecclestone had tried to convince former Brabham driver Niki Lauda out of retirement on the flight back to Europe following the 1985 Australian Grand Prix but to no avail, and then it was thought that Ayrton Senna would be the lead driver when he ran into stumbling blocks in his contract with Lotus. In time however, Senna had his way with the team and so then the rumor mill passed the drive to African-American Willy T. Ribbs. Brabham, as independent as they seemed, were actually very dependent on Italy, with their main sponsor Olivetti, an electronics company, and tire suppliers Pirelli both being Italian. And they got their way. The driver line-up was confirmed as the BT55 was launched on January 20th, 1986, and it would consist of Elio de Angelis and Ricardo Patrese, both Italian and both former Grand Prix winners.

Although the car was completed late, testing soon began in Rio, and quite soon it was understood that the BT55 had some serious shortcomings. The BMW turbo, like many turbo engines of the era, had a reputation for poor drivability. When you have 1400 horsepower at your disposal, it is going to be difficult with any car. This was made worse however by the fact that the BT55 featured less weight on the rear wheels and a narrow track, which caused the "light switch" BMW engine to suffer from great amounts of wheel spin coming out of corners. In addition to wheel spin, the reliability of both the gearbox and the engine were cause for concern, probably because of the way there were titled. It was also discovered that since the engine was tilted, it had oil-scavenging problems with oil pooling in the cylinder and camshaft boxes. This was cutting power out of slow corners and when you consider that "turbo lag" was still a problem in the 1980s, this just made it worse. Additional problems also centered on the cooling of the BMW engine. Since it debuted in 1982, the engine had a reputation for running at high temperatures, a problem that the

Bavarian company never quite overcame. This was a constant problem for the team, even more so now with the BT55. This could have come from the tight confines of the side pods or the tilted engine configuration, or both.

By the time the 1986 season opened at Rio, the team had already made some alterations to the car to help it better accommodate its unusual packaging. The cars were a struggle through practice but actually looked somewhat competitive during the qualifying session. Elio lined up 14th while Pratrese put in a fine performance to start 10th, only to retire after 21 laps with a water leak. de Angelis managed to finish, albeit three laps behind missing two gears, and was classified 8th. He had set the 5th fastest lap of the race though, which showed some promise. Both cars fell out with more gearbox failures in Spain, and in San Marino Elio would qualify back in 19th and fall out with engine failure but Patrese would shine with a 6th place finish, which could have been a podium had he not run out of fuel at the finish. In what would turn out to be his final Grand Prix, de Angelis would have a horrible weekend in Monaco, qualifying 20th after an engine misfire (although Jacques Laffite would actually start last as he wasn't ready for the warm-up lap) and falling out with yet another engine problem, this time with turbo boost problems, while running last on lap 31, while Patrese would put the car a strong 6th on the grid, on a track where the extra down force generated by the wing configuration could be appreciated. It was only to go up away with a fuel pump failure however, on lap 38.

Before the next round of the Championship in Spa, the Brabham team would conduct a testing session at the Paul Ricard Circuit in France. Brabham certainly wasn't alone in the test, as other teams such as Williams, McLaren and Benetton also took part. Brabham were trying to find some speed from the car that had been so disappointing. Although Elio was not known for his technical brilliance or his love for test driving, he was giving it his all in an effort to help the team. Disaster struck when, going into the Verrerie curves, the Brabham suffered a suspected rear wing failure which forced the BT55 into a series of flips that lasted as much as 100 yards, finally coming to rest upside down. The true injustice of this accident is the lack of response from track marshals, as Elio lay trapped in the Brabham for nearly 10 minutes while the car slowly started to burn. Finally, Alan Jones, Nigel Mansell, and Alain Prost arrived at the scene and attempted to turn the car over, but discovered that it was to no avail as the heat was slowly building. A marshal finally arrived on the scene and attempted to put out the fire, but Jones later reviled that most of the spray had gone into the cockpit and not on the fire. But the outrage was not to stop there. After finally being extracted from the cockpit, there was another 30-minute wait for a helicopter to take Elio to a nearby Hospital.

Elio hade suffered a broken collarbone and light burns on his back, but the real problem was the fire in the cockpit that had taken all of Elio's available oxygen away, which eventually proved fatal. The next day, Elio was pronounced dead of massive head and chest injuries at 1:00 PM.

The fatality of de Angelis shocked the entire Brabham team, in particular Murry. de Angelis was a popular and admired Formula One driver, and a winner of two Grand Prixs while driving for Lotus. If anything positive came from this accident, it was that strict safety measures were put forth in the coming years, including the elimination of S-bend where Elio's accident had taken place and the gradual elimination of turbos. The FIA worked quickly to ensure that in the event of an accident, a driver has the best chance for survival possible.

Out of respect to Elio, Brabham only entered one car for the Candian Grand Prix, where Patrese encountered yet more turbo problems. The man who would have to replace Elio would be Englishman Derek Warwick; a man who had been left without a drive after the Renault Elf team had withdrew from Formula One after 1985. He wasn't Italian, but at this point it didn't particularly matter.

In his debut race in Montreal, Warwick qualified 10th, one spot behind Patrese, although both were destined to fall out of the race more BMW failures. The first time that both cars finished came in the United States Grand Prix, where Warwick finished 10th while Patrese scored another point in 6th, which was particularly satisfying when the Brabham was not well suited to acceleration, which is what the tight and twisty motor city track demands.

Both cars again finished when the teams headed back to Paul Ricard for the French Grand Prix, with Patrese only coming up one position shy of the points on the track that had taken his teammate's life. At the British Grand Prix, Brabham actually ran one of the old 1985 BT54 that had been resting in the Donnington Museum for Patrese while keeping Warwick in the BT55 for a comparison. Although Warwick out qualified the BT54 by six positions and lined up ninth, Patrese set a much quicker fast lap in the race before falling out with yet another engine failure and the team were prepared to switch back to the BT54 for the rest of the season. Then came a stumbling block from BMW, who were not able to replace their tilted engine with regular spec, as they were busy supplying Arrows and Benetton. Therefore, like it or not, the BT55 would run for the rest of the year.

The BT55 had its best qualifying performance in Austria when Patrese put the machine fourth on the grid but with Warwick tenth despite crashing at over 200 MPH due to a Pirelli tire failure on Friday. However, there would be only one Brabham starting the race. On race day, Patrese's car arrived on the grid with 2nd and 3rd missing from his gearbox, so he was forced to take Warwick's car since Patrese's spar had been destroyed the previous day because of a turbo fire. All of this effort sadly came to nothing when the BMW experienced another failure after only two laps.

Italy should have suited the car well with Monza's long straights, and Warick did a respectable job to line-up 7th, but would retire from the race when brake problems caused him to spin off. Patrese also crashed out. The only finish the team would be able to record during the final three races would be a 13th in Mexico from Patrese after starting 5th.

The David North and John Baldwin-designed Brabham BT56 that would run in 1987 would be developed almost exclusively from the BT54 and not the BT55, although they would still make use of the lay down engines as all the uprights were sold to the USF&G Company and eventually re-badged as Megatrons following BMW's F1 withdrawal. The BT55 was, in general, an unloved machine and after Elio's accident, totally hated. Gordon Murry later conceded that they had tried too much too quickly, with only an approximate six-month span to get the innovative machine off the ground. Murry would be gone by the end of the 1986 and soon join McLaren, where he, in cooperation with American Steve Nichols, applied what he had learned from the BT55 into the all dominant McLaren MP4/4 which would crush all opposition in 1998, winning 15 of a possible 16 races in the hands of Ayrton Senna and Alain Prost. The low line concept was indeed the right way to go after all.

1989 WEST ZAKSPEED RACING

Chassis: Zakspeed 891
Engine: Yamaha OX88 V8, 3.5-liter normal aspiration
Best Result: DNF (Schneider, Brazil)

THE 1989 ZAKSPEED Yamaha probably is listed for as much the engine as the car, as the Yamaha engine had no business on the track. After years of mediocrity, it was the Zakspeed 891 that finally put the final nail in the coffin of the German F1 team.

Erich Zakowski had decided to run Formula One in 1984, originally trying to use his connections with Ford from his touring car days to secure their new Ford Cosworth turbo charged engine to fit in the back of his first Formula One car in 1985. The Cosworths eventually went the way of the Beatrice Lola team, so Zakowski decided that he would take on the challenge of building both the chassis and 1.5-liter allow block turbo charged flat 4 engine to go with it. Backing came in the form of Reemstma's West Cigarettes, which would be better known in later years for their sponsorship of McLaren. The team was based in Niederzissen, Germany, and Englishman Paul Brown would design the first chassis. Jonathan Palmer was the team's orginial driver but Christian Danner would also driver two races for the team. Throughout 1985 and 1986, the chassis had a reputation for being heavy and bulky, the engine underpowered and unreliable.

Martin Brundle did score two points for the team in 1987, but by 1988 the team was struggling to qualify. The team was also faced with a bit of an engine crisis. Turbochargers (whose boost were now reduced to a new low of 2.5 bar) were to be banned at the end of the season, and the new regulations for 1989 allowed for only 3.5 liter normally aspirated engines. The team had several options, including trying to build their own normally aspirated engine. There were also customer engines available, such as the Ford Cosworth DFR or the Judd. But in the end, Zakspeed chose a surprising route. They entered into an exclusive partnership with Yamaha, a Japanese manufacturer of keyboards and motorcycles. The driver line-up consisted of Bernd Schneider and Arguri Suzuki. Schneider was the 1987 German Formula 3 Champion and had driven for the Zakspeed team in 1988 with his best result being a 12th in his home Grand Prix in Germany with what was basically a year-old car. Suzuki came along with Yamaha and had made his Formula One debut the previous season in a Larrousse Lola as a fill-in for Yanick Dalmas in the Japanese Grand Prix.

Yamaha raised some eyebrows with their F1 involvement because they weren't the traditional car manufacturer or engineering company that usually produces an F1 engine. Their engine was a complex 75-degree V8, which employed a five-valve cylinder and cam, three valves for induction and two for the exhaust, instead of belts. It produced about 10% less horsepower than the customer Fords, and was almost always unreliable. In fact, tests were conducted on the engine to judge the reliability, and one lasted approximately six seconds! Theoretically however, Zakspeed would be better off, not having to worry about the financial or personal resources that building an engine and a car can bring.

Austrian Gustav Brunner, a highly talented and vastly underrated designer who had designed, among others, the infamous Ferrari Indy car and the German F1 efforts of Rial and AGS, designed the 891 with the aid of former Ferrari composite expert Nino Frisson. The machine bared a striking resemblance to the machine that Brunner had constructed for Rial a season earlier. It featured a peculiar airbox as well as incredibly low sidepods. In addition to a new engine, the car would run on different tires, with the team switching from Goodyear to Pirelli.

Although no one was predicting victory heading to Brazil, no one could have expected that the season would be such a total disaster. Because of their poor showings in 1988, the Zakspeed team would have to pre-qualify to get into qualifying. It didn't appear to be a major problem on the Rio circuit as Schneider snuck onto the grid in 25th place, 5.559 seconds off the pole time of Ayrton Senna on an incredibly hot day. Suzuki failed to pre-qualify and was 36th fastest of the 38 cars. Schneider's race was fairly uneventful until a suspension failure resulted in a collision with the Arrows of Eddie Cheever, causing him to retire. Out of the frying pan and into the fire might be a good iconology to describe the rest of the season. The team was incredibly off the pace as Schneider then failed to pre-qualify for the next 13 races, while Suzuki would never escape the pre-qualifying procedure. This included an embarrassing attempt in their home Grand Prix in Germany where the cars were the slowest of 39 entries, with Schneider a massive 8.1 seconds off the pole time of Ayrton Senna with Suzuki taking a shunt into the barriers. The Zakspeed only had enough speed to run with fellow backmarkers Coloni, Euro Brun, and AGS. Schneider was usually faster than Suzuki, who had a couple of massive accidents during the year while attempting to push the machine beyond its limits.

Improvements to the aerodynamics and the chassis, including a revised airbox, came in the middle of the year, but it was to no avail. In August, West announced that, after five years as title sponsor, they would end their support after 1989. Not long afterward, the team was dealt another blow when Brunner left to work under Adrian Newey in the Leyton House/March effort.

The only other time that Schneider would stay through Sunday would come in Suzuka, Japan, which happened to be the home race of Yamaha. Schneider was third fastest in pre-qualifying and then proceeded to beat Benetton, Tyrell, both Arrows, and a Ligier into the 21st spot, which may have caused some hope for the race. That was not to be, as the Zakspeed transverse gearbox gave out on lap one. Only a few occasions, such as the season finale in Australia, Schneider actually posted a time fast enough to qualify, but in typical Schneider luck, he had set his time in pre-qualifying, which wasn't a good enough time to get into actual qualifying. In his final attempt to pre-qualify, Schneider was on his fastest lap until another Yamaha engine failure.

Yamaha withstood a tremendous amount of criticism for this failure and pulled out of Formula One for a year, only to return in 1991 with their OX99 70-degree V12. Schneider would have a quick run in the Arrows in 1990 before bowing out to Italian Alex Caffi, then eventually found success in the German Touring car series. Suzuki would eventually become the only Japanese driver to score a podium when he came third in his home Grand Prix in 1990. And Zakspeed would retreat back to their home in touring cars. Rumors circulated in 1998 that the team, now under the guidance of Peter Zakowski, would re-enter Formula One by purchasing the Arrows team, but this never materialized and it seems that the Zakspeed team and their 1989 failure are consigned to history.

1990 LIFE RACING ENGINES

Chassis: Life F190
Engine: Life F35 W12, 3.5 liter normal aspiration/Judd CV V8,
              3.5 liter normal aspiration
Best Result: 32nd fastest in Pre-Qualifying (Giacomelli, Imola)

DESIGNED FOR "FIRST", but destined for last. The Life F1 team tried to emulate Ferrari with its scarlet red paint and building its own engine. But taking on the Prancing Horse is a tough job, particularly when your car has trouble completing more than two laps at a time.

Perhaps no team in history was as pointless as Life. The late 1980's and early 1990's were infamous for small Italian teams with little or no money attempting to emulate Ferrari and succeed at the sports highest echelon. Some, such as Minardi and Scuderia Italia with their Dallara chassis, were mildly successful, others, such as Andrea Moda and Coloni, were dismal disasters. No team, however, can claim to be as far off the pace or see such little track time as Life Racing Engines.

The man behind this was Italian businessman Ernesto Vita, who formed Life Racing Engines in 1988 with the intent of fielding a Formula One engine for the new 3.5-liter normally aspirated engine formula. He based the small outfit out of Modena, Italy. Despite his enthusiasm, he could not come to terms with any Formula One team to run a Life engine.

In a then-unrelated happening, former Formula One driver Lamberto Leoni's FIRST F3000 team plans to enter in Formula One with their star driver, the talented Gabriele Tarquini. Leoni commissioned Brazilian Richard Divila to design a Formula One car for his FIRST team, which would make use of Judd CV 90-degree V8 engine. Although the car, dubbed the F189, tested with Tarquini, the FIRST team never made it to a Formula One grid and went back to their F3000 duties. Divila was soon off to Ligier to design the JS33 while Tarquini eventually found a drive replacing the injured Philippe Streiff at AGS.

With the FIRST effort dissolved, Vita found an apparently open opportunity to showcase his engines in Formula One and after acquiring the single chassis; Vita hired Gianni Marelli to modify the car to fit the Life engine. That engine being the Life F35, the concept of the late Franco Rocchi, a long time member of the Scuderia Ferrari team. The Life was no ordinary engine, as it was unusual aircraft style W12 cylinder. A W12 differed from a standard V-engine in that instead of two rows of 6 cylinders, the F35 engine was to have 3 rows of four cylinders. The hope was to have the engine as small as a V8 but as powerful as a V12. The power output of the W12 was only 390 horsepower, well down from the top engines. This was the heart of the Life effort, as the hope was to do well enough to convince another team to lease the F35. The car itself, now dubbed the Life F190, featured push rod suspension and the standard airbox on the FIRST car was replaced by a taller version, in addition to two additional air intakes on each side of the driver, which actually wasn't that bad of an idea considering the arrangement of the cylinders. The gearbox was from Life and offered six-speeds. Just as the FIRST had used Goodyear tires during testing, Life would also make use of the American rubber.

Although the car was originally intended to be a test bed for the W12, the F190 was upgraded to pass FIA crash testing and entered the 1990 championship. The team would field only one car, and the driver of choice was Gary Brabham, who was the youngest son of three time World Champion Jack Brabham, and had tested F1 cars for Benetton and Leyton House. Brabham had been signed to a two-year contract.

Their debut was to come in the streets of Phoenix, in the United States, in 1990. Because Life was a new team they would have to participate in pre-qualifying for at least the first few races of the season.

Throughout practice and into pre-qualifying, Brabham suffered several engine problems. When you consider that Life only had two engine blocks at their disposal and only one chassis, it only added to their struggle. It seems as if Life was so ill prepared for Formula One that the life mechanics had to borrow tools from other teams! A constant misfire that eventually resulted in an engine failure after four laps meant that by the end of the session, Brabham was ranked 33rd out of the 35 cars. That fact is a little misleading when you consider that J.J. Letho's Oynx Ford did not have a recorded time and Bertrand Gachot's Coloni Subaru encountered problems and failed to record a time that was under 5 minutes. Brabham was a full 38.403 seconds off the pole time of Gerhard Berger in his McLaren Honda. Furthermore, he was 29.668 seconds slower than Claudio Langes's Euro Brun Judd, the next slower qualifier. Additional problems in the next round in the championship in Brazil mean that Brabham didn't even post a time after completing only 400 meters before another W12 gave up the ghost. After realizing that Life were hopelessly off the pace even the worst Formula One cars, and no finances to improve the situation, Brabham did the smart thing and left the team, albeit in disgust. Even still, the young Australian had lost the money he had spent on the flights to the United States and Brazil. Brabham would never drive in official competition again, but would occasionally test Formula One cars.

It didn't take Life long to find a replacement, and an impressive one at that. The team selected Italian Bruno Giacomelli, who had driven for Formual One teams such as McLaren, Alfa Romeo, and Toleman in the late 1970's and early 1980's. So when he wasn't developing things such as active suspension with the powder blue Leyton Houses, he would have the task of attempting to take the reluctant Life machine to a qualifying position. Giacomelli made his debut in Imola, but like Brabham before him, got little track time. The team continued to have problems with its W12 engine, and rarely got more than a few laps of running in before difficulties sent it back to the pit lane. His official time around the circuit was 7 minutes and 16.212 seconds, only 5 minutes and 52.992 seconds off pole! The closest that Bruno ever came to actually pre-qualifying the car was in Monte Carlo. Monaco is a circuit that is legendary for allowing a better driver to make up for his lesser machinery, which is perhaps why Giacomelli was only 19.873 seconds off pole time. On the upside, he was only two seconds slower than the equally disappointing Coloni of Betrand Gachot, powered by a 12 cylinder Subaru. By now, the pitlane was filled with jokes of "the engine with no Life".

Results similar to these continued for the rest of Life's duration. The car, when it was able to complete a lap, usually ran 20-30 seconds off pole time. In the summer of 1990, Vita sold the majority of the team to Verona industrialist Daniele Battaglino, as the two had come to terms supply racecars to a Leningrad engineering company.

Finally, perhaps in an act of desperation, after the Italian Grand Prix Life deserted their own engine and started using the Judd V8, which the car had, originally been designed for. Although a significant power gain was achieved, these were old, outdated engines that had formally belonged to Lotus during the previous year. The Judd had actually been competitive in the back of the Williams and the March/Leyton Houses, but overall they were not regarded as one of the better engines and they certainly not able to transform Life. When the Judd was installed in the back of the F190, the engine cover, one of the things that Life had modified from the original chassis, wouldn't fit properly. Not surprisingly, they didn't record a time in Portugal after lingering electrical problems, and in what turned out to be their final Grand Prix, were 24.312 seconds off pole time in Spain after Giacomelli managed only two laps in pre-qualifying.

Out of money, out of parts and clearly out of their league, Life would withdraw after the European season ended, not wanting to spend the money to fly around the world just to fail to pre-qualify. Plans to compete in 1991 under the ownership of Battaglino with additional backing from Russian syndicate eventually fell through and thus Life Racing Engines would never attempt a Grand Prix again. And not surprisingly, no team was interested in the F35.

1992 ANDREA MODA FORMULA

Chassis: Coloni C4/Moda S921
Engine: Judd GV V10, 3.5-liter normal aspiration
Best Result: DNF (Moreno, Monaco)

SHOULD ANYONE LOOK for an example of just what a struggle Formula One can be, then one should look no further than the display put forth by Andrea Moda Formula in 1992. Andrea Moda, with Andrea Sassetti at the helm, is generally considered by most people to be the least professional Formula One team ever.

Andrea Moda was created from the ashes of the old Coloni team, which included a number of ex-Coloni employees. After five years of struggling, Enzo Coloni had finally given up trying to crack the F1 nut and had sold his team to Italian businessman Andrea Sassetti. Sassetti made his fortune in the selling of shoes in his native Italy his Andrea Moda shoe empire, but his F1 adventures were always on the wrong foot, if you will.

Coloni had used their C4 chassis in 1991, fitted with the traditional customer Ford Cosworth DFR engine. The car was updated version of the machine that had struggled in 1990 and had failed to pre-qualify with Pedro Chaves and Nakio Hattori in 1991. For at least the first race, the Andrea Moda team would have to use what was nearly a two-year-old design that was not competitive when it debuted. Sassetti had replaced the Cosworth with customer Judd GV 72-degree V10s and now were getting their gearboxes from Dallara. Tires, like every runner that year, were supplied by Goodyear.

The original driver line-up was scheduled to be the Italian duo of

Alex Caffi and Enrico Bertaggia (the later having a short stint in the previous Coloni team), who were to attempt to qualify the old C4 chassis in the season opener in South Africa. However, in the days leading up to the race, there was a dispute between Andrea Moda and the race organizers whether the Andrea Moda team should have been considered a new team and required to pay the $100,000 new team fee. Sassetti's argument was that Andrea Moda was not totally a new team and therefore should not be required to pay the fee. Sassetti had precedent on his side, as teams like March had become Leyton House and back to March and Osella had become Fondmetal. These teams had exchanged ownership but were not considered new teams. However, Andrea Moda was a new team but still using the Coloni chassis, and part of the Concorde agreement states that a team be responsible for its own design. To add to this, the Coloni was also facing the strict crash testing by the FIA. The race organizers did not agree with Sassetti's argument, and after Caffi did a few demonstration laps on Thursday before encountering problems, the team left South Africa without participating in qualifying.

Sassetti never took the team to Mexico, as it was certain they would again be disqualified, which went against F1 regulations insisting that team appear at every Grand Prix. It was then that Caffi, who was actually quite highly rated just a few years before, left the team and Bertaggia had fallen out of favor with team management and was released. Brazilian Roberto Moreno and Englishman Perry 'Pel' McCarthy filled their places. Moreno had driven for numerous low budget Formula One teams before getting a real chance in late 1990 when Benetton driver Sandro Nannini lost his arm in a helicopter crash. Although his arm would be reattached, he would never drive a Formula One car in competition again. Moreno came a fine second in Japan to teammate Nelson Piquet and would get the second seat at Benetton full time in 1991, but following the Belgian Grand Prix in Spa (where he recorded fast lap), he was replaced by a young Michael Schumacher. McCarthy had driven in the American IMSA series with great success in 1991 with Spice, and then in 1992 with Nissan.

But better things were supposedly on the horizon as Sassetti had arranged for the team to enter its own car, the S921. The basic chassis was the work of Nick Wirth, who had completed the car in secret as a project for BMW as the German giant had considered returning to the Formula One arena, only to change their minds. Wirth was head of the Simtek Research firm, thus the "S" in the chassis's name. A single S921 was entered for Moreno is his home Grand Prix in Brazil, but the Brazilian was the slowest qualifier after a troubled weekend and failed to make the starting grid. McCarthy had been present in Brazil, but had his super license revoked before turning a lap.

From the beginning it was obvious that McCarthy was the one who would suffer the worst. The team had only two chassis available most of the time, and usually the second chassis was reserved as a spare for Moreno. This meant that McCarthy would see little, if any, serious practice on race weekends. Before Spain, there was actually an attempt to replace McCarthy with Bertaggia, who had apparently found more funds that interested the cash strapped team. This time, however, the FIA denied the team another driver change, so McCarthy found himself back in the team.

In qualifying for the Spanish Grand Prix, Moreno was 16.965 seconds off pole time set by Nigel Mansell's Williams Renault. Furthermore, he was 9.392 seconds off the next slowest qualifier, Damon Hill's Brabham Judd. McCarthy, in what would be an all too frequent occurrence, would not post a time. In fact, he traveled a mere 18 yards before his Judd engine stalled, fueling rumors that there was no engine at all in the car and that engine noises were made by the crew.

Monaco, true to its reputation for an odd result, was to be the only race the team ever successfully qualified for. Moreno, who most people feel was vastly underrated, out ran Ukyo Katayama's Venturi Lamborghini in pre-qualifying. Then he did the impossible by outqualifying the Brabham Judds of Eric van de Poele and Damon Hill, the Fondmetal of Andrea Chiesa, and the year-old March CG911 of Paul Belmondo for the last spot on the grid. But in the race, Moreno retired after only 11 of the 78 laps when his Judd fell silent.

Somewhat surprisingly, Moreno was quite competitive at the high-speed Hockenheim track, only to suffer an engine failure and missing the chance to pre-qualify by only three tenths of a second.

Much of what befell the team could be blamed on their own actions, but it should be said that luck was not on their side. For instance, at the Canadian Grand Prix in Montreal, the team's engines never arrived. A severe storm had caused the British Airways flight that was carrying the Judds to unload all cargo, and without computer assistance to balance the load properly, the V10s were left setting on the terminal. Moreno managed a couple of laps using a borrowed engine from Brabham, but of course, he never qualified. 1992 represented the year of the French lorry drivers' strike, which blocked all major roads in France. This meant that Andrea Moda would even have a chance making the field yet again. In August, at the Hungarian Grand Prix, the team was warned by the FIA to improve efforts to provide suitable cars for both drivers to qualify or they faced possible exclusion from the Championship.

In Spa, McCarthy was going through the Eau Rouge turn when the steering locked because the chassis was flexing so severely. When informing the team of his troubles, they revealed that they knew of the problem as they had taken the steering off Moreno's car at the previous race! Moreno and McCarthy were again last in 28th and 29th position (Eric Comas's Ligier Renault did not record a time). At the same time, Sassetti was arrested in the paddock for allegedly forging invoices. By now, Sassetti was counting his substantial loses and by the time the Italian Grand Prix came around, the team found themselves unwelcome in the Formula One paddock, as the FIA had finally laid down the law, banning the team from competing for the duration of the championship. Plans to enter the 1993 championship fell apart during the winter. This was the end of Andrea Moda.

1994 PACIFIC GRAND PRIX LTD

Chassis: Pacific PR01
Engine: Ilmor V10, 3.5-liter normal aspiration
Best Result: DNF (Belmondo, Monaco)

FORMULA ONE HAS always been at the cutting edge of automotive technology. What is acceptable one year might be obsolete the next. Just to keep up takes massive amounts of funding. This is why the 1994 Pacific failed; using what was in effect a stillborn chassis design along with two-year-old engines with virtually no money to speak of.

Adrian Reynard had a dream. That dream was to enter Formula One. The late 1980s saw as many as 39 cars attempt a Grand Prix, and Reynard felt that he was more than capable of making it on to the grid as well. Reynard had built his first racecar in 1973, and had since grown the company with steady progress. Reynard got serious about his F1 aspirations by hiring Benetton designer Rory Byrne to design the car, which Reynard hoped would take him to the Formula One grid. Developmental pieces that were destined for the F1 car were first tested on the Reynard F3000 car being ran by Madgwick Motorsports.

Yet there were stumbling blocks. For one, Reynard had problems coming up with adequate sponsorship. The early 1990s were not the best time to ask a company to sponsor a racing car. Much of the world was in a recession and even mid-field teams had trouble finding enough sponsorship. Another would be the engine. Byrne knew that in order to have a suitable aerodynamic package the car would need to have generally small sidepods, but the engines available were not exactly able to withstand large amounts of heat. With such huge sidepods, the car would never have worked. Therefore, the project was eventually shelved and the debts nearly bankrupted Reynard. Byrne soon headed back to Benetton, and Reynard eventually set his attention to Indy Cars, debuting in 1994 and soon becoming the dominant chassis. Reynard would eventually enter Formula One with British American Racing in 1999.

But we had not heard the last of the stillborn Formula One design. Enter Keith Wiggins, head of the Pacific race team. Wiggins's team had won the F3000 Championship in 1991 and he had desperately tried to enter Formula One in 1992, but to no avail. A similar situation happened in 1993 when Wiggins actually signed on to use customer Ford Cosworth V8s. But this was another doomed attempt as more financial problems doomed the attempt yet again.

But 1994 was to mark the official entry of Pacific Grand Prix. Wiggins would be running on a shoestring budget, therefore picking up the Reynard design. In addition to the car, Wiggins had agreed to terms with Ilmor Engineering to run 1992 spec V10s, which had previously powered Tyrrell and March. These engines would account for nearly 40% of the team's budget, but with Ilmor paying most of its attention to its new relationship with Mercedes-Benz, these engines would see minimal development through the season. The PR01 would have a distinct "shark" nose, similar to the Benettons, which is not surprising considering Byrne had designed both cars. The gearbox offered a sequential 6-speed. The Pacific team were no different than any other 1994 runner in that they were supplied with Goodyear tires.

The driver line-up would feature Bertrand Gachot and Paul Belmondo. Gachot had showed some promise driving for Jordan in 1991, setting fastest lap in Hungry, but his career had tailed off and after a disappointing year at Larrousse in 1992, he would be not only the lead driver but a stock holder in the Pacific team. Belmondo had driven for March while they were on their last legs in 1992 and had tested for Benetton in 1993, but had never been particularly impressive, but he did come with some sponsorship that was of interest to Pacific.

To begin with, there were some problems with the initial installation of the Ilmor engine. When preseason testing finally got underway, the team suffered numerous engine failures, leading to allegations that Ilmor were giving Pacific used parts. It was also discovered that the car was extremely difficult to drive, and had a horrible aerodynamic capabilities. There were also severe problems with the chassis itself being too weak.

Ready or not, the Pacific team would make their debut in the season opening Brazilian Grand Prix. Both drivers complained of a severe oversteer problem in the opening practice session, along with wheelspin and trouble selecting the proper gear ratios. In the first day of qualifying, Belmondo's clutch failed on the first lap out while Gachot was 26th fastest. Belmondo encountered yet more problems on the second day since parts were at premium, he failed to post a time, while Gachot made it into the race in 25th position, out qualifying fellow F1 newcomers Simtek with David Brabham.

In the race, Gachot was out on a lap once after a collision with Olivier Beretta's Larrousse. Despite the fact that Belmondo didn't qualify and Gachot had crashed out on the first lap, the Pacific's had completed more laps during the weekend than in all of preseason testing.

The next Grand Prix was the Pacific Grand Prix, not because of Pacific, but to allow more than one race in Japan. The Pacific's both encountered engine problems on Friday, and both still complained of a lack of traction, particularly out of slow corners. On Saturday, more problems meant that Belmondo would give up his car in the final minutes of qualifying to allow Gachot a few laps around the circuit. It didn't help, as Bertrand found his teammates car uncomfortable. Although Gachot did better Belmondo's time by seven tenths of a second, it was not enough to qualify. Both cars were well off the pace and had to go home on Saturday.

Before the next round at San Marino, the team conducted a test at

Mugello, where they concentrated on, among other things, reliability and improving traction.

The 1994 San Marino Grand Prix will live in infamy for as long as Grand Prix cars take to the grid. On Friday, Rubens Barrichello endured a massive accident where his car went into the railing. The Brazilian's condition appeared serious, but he would indeed survive and live to race – and win – another day.

On Saturday, Simtek rookie Roland Ratzenberger suffered damage to his front wing during qualifying which would become fatal when the wing broke and the Austrian slammed into the retaining wall, probably killing him instantly.

Then on race day, Grand Prix superstar and three time World Champion Ayrton Senna was killed when his Williams went off in the Tamberello corner.

And while no one was really watching, the Pacific's were still struggling. Gachot made it on the grid in 25th and if the race stewards had decided to take Ratzenberger's time out of the session, it would have allowed Belmondo into the field. That did not happen however, and Gachot fell out on lap 23 after another Ilmor engine failure resulting from a loss of oil pressure.

Tragedy would see to it that two Pacific's made it to the grid in Monaco. Out of respect for Senna and Ratzenberger, Williams and Simtek only entered one car apiece. Then in free practice on Thursday, Karl Windlinger's Sauber Mercedes hit the barrier just after the tunnel. Windlinger would sustain massive injuries and lie in a coma for 19 days but would live. Sauber however, would withdraw both cars from the race. This meant that Gachot and Belmondo would line up 23rd and 24th despite numerous engine problems. In the race, Gachot was conservative, just wanting to finish. It appeared to be working until lap 49 of the 78-lap race, when his gearbox seized. Belmondo might have actually finished, but after 53 laps, pulled into the pits complaining of numbness and cramps in his right foot and both arms.

With Wendlinger still clinging to life, Sauber did not field a second car in Spain, therefore assuring Pacific of at least one car in the race. But once again, another team;s misfortunes would aid Pacific. Andrea

Montermini, who was suffering from the flu, would have a violent crash in his Simtek on the final corner of the Barcelona circuit. In fairness to Gachot and Belmondo, they had both been faster than Montermini in practice, as the Italian was in his first race for the Simtek team. Although Montermini would suffer foot injuries, it was nothing serious but he would not be able to race. This meant that for the second race in a row, two Pacifics would start the race.

At the start, Gachot ran over a curb, which eventually caused the rear wing to crack, ending his race after 32 laps. Belmondo had already retired after only 2 laps, locking up the car under braking and spinning into the sand. But both drivers had said that the car had performed better throughout the weekend.

In Canada, Andrea de Cesaris was put into the second Sauber, but now the grid was minus Montermini as Simtek only ran one car. Therefore a Pacific was again guaranteed to make the race. As expected, the battle for the final qualifying position was between the two Pacific drivers. It was close, but Gachot managed to beat Belmondo to the spot by two tenths of a second. In the race, Gachot managed to complete 47 laps before oil pressure problems put him out. This would be the final time that a Pacific made the grid in 1994.

Gachot came close to qualifying in France, missing the mark by only a tenth of a second to Jean-Marc Gounon, while Belmondo was over a second off Gachot on his home Grand Prix.

The rest of the year was a broken record for the team. Gachot was usually faster than Belmondo but too slow to race. The team did try to improve the PR01, most notably replacing the shark nose with a drop nose. But it did little good. Both Gachot and Belmondo were vocal of the car, which was slow and hard to drive, and its engine, which was down on power and unreliable. Belmondo summed up the shortcomings of the Pacific team after the final qualifying session of the season, "The PR01 was a car which required you to look in the mirrors if you wanted a clear lap – hopefully next year I'll have a car which allows me to concentrate on the track in front..." Gachot then made the statement "Today is a great day because I will never have to drive the PR01 again! It really has been a very difficult season for us all because of the uncompetitiveness of this car, but morale has remained high and the team's motivation never wavered."

It should be stated that if Pacific had their way, they probably would have bowed out when it was obvious the car didn't have the speed to qualify, but the ever-stricter entry rules meant that if the team wanted to return in 1995, they would have to attend all the races.

The 1994 Pacific represents a lesson that no matter how bad one wants something; they must come in prepared and not let their hearts overshot their heads. Pacific desperately wanted to run in Formula One, but they would have been wiser to come in only when they had adequate backing and a suitable engine and chassis program.

1997 MASTER CARD LOLA F1 TEAM

Chassis: Lola T97/30
Engine: Ford EC V8, 3.0-liter normal aspiration
Best Result: DNQ (Sospiri, Australia)

WHEN A TEAM enters modern Grand Prix Racing, they need to be ready. They need to have the proper sponsorship, testing, a suitable amount of time to develop, and realistic goals. Lola Cars thought they could enter Formula One in 1997 with virtually none of these. After such high hopes for the car, the results were one race where both cars failed to qualify within the 107% rule and a financial crisis that brought the once proud company to its knees.

Eric Broadley founded Lola Cars 1958, building a MK1 Sports Car. He then proceeded to make Lola one of the world's most respected racecar manufacturers for four decades. Lola have won the Indy Car Championship six times, in addition to three Indianapolis 500 wins. They also entered into a partnership with Ford to design the gorgeous GT-40s that won the 24 Hours of Le Mans four years in a row, from 1966 to 1969 They have also supplied support series such as the International Formula 3000 series and Indy Lights with spec racing cars.

Lola also has a Formula One background. In 1962, Reg Parnell commissioned an F1 car from Lola for drivers John Surtees and Roy Salvadori, with Surtess finishing second at Silverstone and the Nurburgring while also taking pole position at the Dutch Grand Prix. In 1967, Surtess again teamed with Lola with the support and engine power coming from Honda to race the RA300/T130, which won the Italian Grand Prix at Monza. Although Honda would withdraw from Formula One the following season, Lola's F1 experience was far from over. Over the next 25 years, Lola would enter into partnerships with such teams as Embassy Hill, Larrousse, and the BMS Scuderia Italia team.

But none of these efforts were from the Lola factory. Lola would build and develop the cars while the team would actually run the operation. It was, in effect, a "customer" chassis, similar to customer engines. Broadley wanted more. In the mid 1990s, rumors had Lola running their own factory Formula One team. In fact, a Formula One prototype had been tested with Alan McNish doing the driving. But Broadly would need adequate sponsorship, and he thought he had found it with the MasterCard Company. In November 1996, an agreement was reached for MasterCard to be the title sponsorship of the new Lola Grand Prix team. But the MasterCard sponsorship was not your ordinary arrangement of spending money in exchange for advertisement on the car. MasterCard had developed a program where MasterCard holders could be involved in a fan club of sorts, with a portion of the proceeds handed over to the Formula One team. There were three sponsorship levels ranging from $79 to $2,999. In return, a fan would receive rewards ranging from a newsletter, race team merchandise and apparel, and even dinner with the team and drivers. As much as $10 million could be raised for the team using this bizarre method of sponsorship payment.

Broadley had wanted to enter Formula One in 1998, but in the end of the board of directors and MasterCard demanded that the team debut in 1997. This would mean that the team would have fully constructed their car, the T97/30, in three months. The car would originally be fitted with customer Ford Cosworth V8s, but Lola had painned to have their own Lola V10, built by MCD Consultants, on the grid by mid season. MCD boss Al Melling had already built an engine and tested it on the dyno.

The driver line-up was announced in mid-December and would consist of F3000 standouts Vincenzo Sospiri and Ricardo Rosset, who as teammates had finished one-two the 1995 F3000 Championship.

Sospiri was a Benetton test driver while Rosset had spent a year with Footwork/Arrows and came with personal sponsorship from Lycra and Safra. Ray Bourter was hired as the general manager of the effort.

In addition to the short amount of time the team had to prepare for the first round in Australia, Lola, like all teams, faced the new 107% rule in qualifying. The 107% meant that any team that hoped to start the race would have to qualify within 107% of the fastest time. This was put in place to make sure that a truly slow car was not allowed to start the race and become a hazard. Broadley felt his team would have no problem with this rule and stated: "The 107% rule is actually quite a large margin. If we can't do that, then we really shouldn't be in it."

The cars were barley shaken down before the opening around and have never even seen a wind tunnel. In practice; Lola suffered various problems including balance and electronic struggles and were well behind the rest of the field. In qualifying, the cars were hopelessly off the pace, with Rosset over 12.7 seconds behind and Sospiri 11.6 seconds off pole time. They were nowhere near the 107% cut off and although Pedro Dinz's Arrows also didn't make it, some protesting by Arrows boss Tom Walkinshaw, Dinz was allowed to start the race.

The team knew they had a lot of work facing them if they were to qualify in the next round in Brazil. A test at Silverstone had the team testing new suspension setups as well as doing extensive work on the electronics in an effort to find speed. But the team still had not received any money from the MasterCard program and Ford needed money for engine revisions to their Ecs.

The team arrived in Brazil with still no money from MasterCard. By now, the Lola F1 program had built up millions of dollars in debt, some of which was owed to parent company Lola Cars. With no money to speak of, the team returned to headquarters without delay without ever turning a lap on the Interlogos Circuit, and so the Lola team was gone. Sospiri is still convinced that they could have qualified in Brazil, had they had the opportunity.

A few days later, Lola officially announced their withdraw from the Championship citing *"financial and technical reasons"*. There were rumors of a comeback by the San Marino Grand Prix, but they were just that, rumors.

Lola Cars very nearly folded that year, with the entire company in financial ruin. It didn't help that the Indy Car chassis suffered from severe aero pitch sensitivity and had been deserted by all its customers by the end of the season. Martin Birrane eventually purchased Lola and sent it through major financial restructing. The company eventually bounced back and is again producing open wheel and sports car chassis, but another attempt at Formula One seems unlikely at best.

1999 BRITISH AMERICAN RACING

Chassis: BAR 01
Engine: Supertec FB01 V10, 3.0-liter Normal Aspiration
Best Result: 7th (Villeneuve, three times, Salo, San Marino)

IT HAS BEEN said that no team has did so little with so much as the British American Racing team in 1999. For a team that expected to win their first race, not scoring a point all year must have been hard to bear.

The concept for BAR was born the day after the 1995 Indy 500. Jacques Villeneuve had just won what would be the final Indy 500 under the CART banner and appeared to be off to Formula One. Craig Pollock, a long time friend and manager of Villeneuve, and Adrian Reynard, the owner of the company that manufactured Villeneuve's winning car, are generally the ones credited with the concept of fielding an F1 team and possibly building it around Villeneuve. Pollock proposed the plan to British American Tobacco, the largest manufacture of cigarettes on Earth. In late 1997, British American Tobacco purchased Ken Tyrrell's F1 team. The team was a front-runner in the 1970s' but had fallen on hard times and 1998 would be the final year under the Tyrrell name. Villeneuve had won the 1997 World Championship but Williams had produced a less competitive car in 1998, so he announced in mid season that he would leave the Williams team to become the team's number one driver, and after much speculation, F3000 sensation and McLaren test driver Ricardo Zonta would drive the team's second car. The team also announced that they would receive their engines from Supertec Sport, headed by ex-Benetton boss

Flavio Briatore. The Supertec V10 was nothing more than a rebadged Mecachrome engine, which was actually a two year old ex works Renault engine. The engines were still available at a cost of approximately $20 million a year. The engine's age had began to show during 1998, and considering there was only minimal improvement for 1999, BAR would not have a power advantage over many of their competitors. BAR were the company's third team, along with Benetton and Williams. After an initial test with the old Tyrrell chassis fitted with a Supertec, the BAR team then officially made its testing debut with the BAR 01 on December 15, 1998.

British American Tobacco was no stranger to Formula One. Many of the companies' brands, such as John Player Special and Barclay, had seen Formula One involvement before. But this was the first time that they would own the team. It sounded like a good idea for a tobacco giant, especially when you consider the ever-stricter regulations facing cigarette advertisement. In addition to owning the team, BAT would supply over $60 million annually in sponsorship fees to the team, which made BAR's first year budget over $80 million, a large budget for any team, but especially when you consider this was their debut year. The original marketing plan for the team was a bizarre approach by having different sponsors on the two cars. It is written in the FIA rulebook that for each two car Formula Once team, they are to have both cars look approximately the same. This was against the powers that be at BAR, and they had the nerve to actually file a lawsuit against the governing body in December 1998. BAT would launch their car on January 6th, 1999, with Villeneuve's car painted in Lucky Strike livery, while Zonta's showed allegiance to the 555 brand. A clear violation of the rules. It was also at the team's launch, which was attended by over 500 members of the media, that Adrian Reynard made the infamous quote "I have no reason to believe we can't win our first race".

Of course, the FIA is not intimidated by anyone, and BAR was no exception. The FIA ruled that both cars had to have the same livery. That meant that BAR would have to decide on one tobacco livery. Well not exactly, because on February third, the BAR team unveiled what

Formula One Famous Failures | *Matthew Teaters*

came to be known as "the zipper car". One side wore the 555 livery, while the other was dedicated to the Lucky Strike branding, with a yellow zipper deal ran down the middle of the car separating the two color schemes. Not exactly idea, but this was a way that both cigarette brands would get the exposure they had originally intended.

In preseason testing, BAR had a lot of problems with the new car, particularly with the gearbox. It was not well suited to handle the Supertec engine, which was heavy and caused a lot of vibration throughout the car. In general, the BAR Reynard 01, which was designed by Australian Malcolm Oastler, designer of Reynard's Champ Car and F3000 chassis, as well as being under the supervision of Adrian Reynard, was built fairly light and fragile, so the problems the Supertec engine created were made more noticeable than for Benetton and Williams.

When the team finally arrived in Australia, they learned very quickly that a win in their first race was not likely. McLaren and Ferrari were still the class of the field, and along with Benetton and Williams, BAR complained of a distinct lack of power from their engine. When the qualifying session ended, Jacques Villeneuve had turned the 11th fastest time, 2.426 seconds off pole time, while Zonta lined up 19th, 3.950 seconds back. In the race, Villeneuve ran competitively until suffering a rear wing failure on the 13th lap which caused a 180 MPH spin, while Zonta continued on until another gearbox failure put him out on lap 48, only nine laps from the end. It was unclear whether BAR had created a flexible rear wing to allow for higher straightway speed, or whether the vibrations caused from the Supertec engine had caused the wing to fall off, but it should be noted that Benetton suffered a similar failure in off-season testing using the same engine.

In Brazil, things were not about to get any better. Zonta, in his home Grand Prix, had an accident a practice session and broke a bone in his foot, putting him out of action. Villeneuve was later disqualified from his 16th qualifying position because of a fuel infraction and forced to line-up 21st and last on the grid. Villeneuve fell out of the race when his hydraulics failed on lap 49.

BAR now had to find a replacement for Zonta. The most obvious choice was Mika Salo, the talented Finnish driver who had lost his drive from the Arrows team only weeks before the season opener. In addition, Salo was also a close friend of Jacque Villeneuve. Therefore, Salo would drive for the team until Zonta was fully recovered.

The third round of the Formula One season was notable for giving BAR its best qualifying position all year. In a brilliant performance, Jacques Villeneuve put the BAR 01 solidly on the third row, in fifth position, only .951 seconds behind Mika Hakkinen's pole time. Salo, still new to the car, lined up 19th. But the race was somewhat symbolic of BAR's entire season when Villeneuve never even got off the line, suffering gearbox failure. Salo actually finished the race, albeit three laps down, in seventh position. It was to be the best result the team would register all season. Neither car would finish in Monaco, Villeneuve out with an oil leak while Salo officially retired with brake failure, which caused him to slide off the road.

The Spanish Grand Prix was possibly the highlight of the Grand Prix season. Villeneuve put in another tremendous performance to get the car an amazing sixth on the starting line, only .615 seconds off pole. Then he made an incredible start to vault past Michael Schumacher's Ferrari and run a stellar third for the first half of the race, holding off the far superior Ferrari until the first round of pit stops. But by lap 40, Villeneuve suffered yet another gearbox failure, while Salo dragged his machine home in eighth, a lap down.

The next round in Canada was, as always, very special for Villeneuve. Not only is it his home Grand Prix, but also the circuit, Circuit de Gilles Villeneuve, is named after his late father Gilles. Canda also marked the return of Zonta, following an FIA medical test, was declared fit to race. That is why it was disappointing to see the cars line-up only 16th and 17th on the grid, and both would crash out on race day.

By the time that the British Grand Prix had rolled around in July, the team had still not scored but the events of the race would take some of the media spotlight away from BAR's failure. On the first lap of the race, Michael Schumacher suffered a broken leg when his car suffered a brake failure. Ferrari would call on the same man who had replaced Zonta at BAR, Mika Salo. But this was apparently a problem for BAR, as they eventually field a lawsuit against Salo's management for the money that Salo earned during his time with the BAR team. It was another black eye for the first year team.

The Belgium Grand Prix qualifying session was perhaps the darkest day for the team. First Villeneuve, attempting to go flat out through the infamous Eau Rouge turn, lost control and flipped violently end over end. What was most amazing, however, was that Villeneuve was not only unhurt, but ran back to the pits to get the spare car! Then, in an amazing twist of fate, Zonta also lost control of his machine in the same turn and had an accident almost identical to Villeneuve's! In order to have two functioning racecars for race day, the team had to redirect the test team to Belgium. The team would achieve a small victory on Sunday, with Villeneuve making it across the finish line foe the first time all year, albeit in 15th place. This is the same man who had won the World Championship only two years earlier and had won the pole in his first grand prix.

The team finished out the final races of the 1999 season, with now all attention being paid to he BAR 02, which would run in the year 2000. Oastler felt that the design of the BAR 01 was sound, but made for too fragile, thus the BAR 02 would be a development of the BAR 01.

The biggest accomplishment of the team during 1999 occurred off the track. After leaving their agreement with Supertec a year early, BAR announced a three-year partnership with Honda for supply of the works Honda V10 during the 2000 season as well as help in chassis development.

2000 GULOISES PROST PEUGEOT

Chassis: ProstAP03
Engine: Peugeot A20 V10, 3.0-liter normal aspiration
Best Result: 8th Heidfeld, Monaco)

THE 2000 SEASON was supposed to be different for Frenchman Alain Prost's team. Additional sponsorship and a new Peugeot engine had raised hopes that the French team would finally have their break through season. But it was not to be. In fact, the 2000 season was a disaster that Alain would like to forget.

Alain Prost was a four time World Champion and winner of 51 Grand Prix before he bought the Ligier team from Flavio Briatore just before the start of the 1997 season. Ligier had been a fixture of the Grand Prix scene since Guy Ligier had originally entered Formula One in 1975. Through the years the team had varied success and failure, but was now a mid field runner.

It is fair to say that the only successful Prost wasn't really a Prost at all. The 1997 Prost was simply the Ligier JS45, which in all honesty was a development of the 1995 title winning Benetton. It was fitted with the Mugen-Honda engine, which was basically an ex works Honda engine that was being supplied through Mugen. The car was quick at times and Jarno Trulli nearly won in Austria before an engine failure put him out. But it was understood from the beginning that the Mugens would be replaced in 1998 with the Peugeot factory engine. In 1912 Peugeot had revolutionized Grand Prix racing with its introduction of the twin-cam four-valve engine, then went on to win the Indianapolis 500 in 1913, 1916, and 1919, and the 24 hours of Le Mans in 1992 and 1993. The company entered Formula One in 1994 with McLaren and had spent the last three years with Jordan, with some success. Now they would partner a team of their own nationality, no doubt a major influence behind the partnership.

The AP01 was severely overweight and only scored one point during 1998, and while the AP02 was much better in terms of aerodynamics, it still suffered weight problems and scored nine points in 1999, six of which were scored by Jarno Trulli's second place finish in a bizarre European Grand Prix at the Nurburgring, Peugeot became disinterested in the project and soon a war of words between the French car manufacturer and the Prost team erupted, each blaming the other for the lack of success. It was a surprise to some that the Peugeot partnership continued into the year 2000, the third and final year of their agreement.

The AP03 was to be a giant leap forward in terms of technology. Critic's thought of the AP02 as being too conservative, thus the AP03 would be a virtually new car inside and out. Three men did the majority of the work on the design of the AP 03, John Bernard, Alan Jenkins, and Luic Bigios. The car featured a seven-speed gearbox, periscope exhausts which the team had debuted in the 1999 Italian Grand Prix, entirely new electronics from TAG, a lower center of gravity achieved by lowering the seating position and forward portion of the chassis, including a complete re-packaging of the torsion spring and damper package. But perhaps most importantly the AP03 would feature an entirely new Peugeot engine, the A20, which would replace the A18 whose design dated back to the 1997 season. The A20 featured an improved power output of approximately 790 horsepower, but more importantly it was lower, lighter, and shorter than its predecessor. In fact, when the new A20 could not even fit into the AP02 in post 1998 season testing. In addition, the Prost team adopted common oil circuits for both the car and the engine. Prost had enjoyed a tight relationship with Bridgestone ever since the tire manufacturer had purchased on old Ligier to use as a test vehicle and the AP03, like every other car on the grid, ran on the Japanese rubber.

The Prost team also had more funding to start the 2000 season, enticing Internet giant Yahoo! To become a secondary sponsor alongside longtime title sponsor Gualioses, a French manufacturer of cigarettes. The Yahoo! sponsorship was to be for three years with a reported $8 million annually to be paid to the French team.

The driver line-up would also be promising. Frenchman Jean Alesi had left the Sauber team to become Prost's number one driver. Alesi was long regarded as a man with top talent but through bad judgment and bad luck, had managed only one career win that coming in the 1995 Canadian Grand Prix with Ferrari. Prost and Alesi were close friends and had even been teammates during their stint at Ferrari in 1991. Partnering Alesi would be German Nick Heidfeld, the reining F3000 Champion who was on loan from McLaren. Talent in the driving department would not be in question.

But preseason testing did not go as planned. The car hardly completed a race distance and encountered numerous problems with the Peugeot engine, which was suffering from reliability problems. Peugot's traditional way of improving reliability was simply reducing the revolutions until the engine didn't explode, hardly encouraging development. Peugeot also had what was generally considered an outdated design philosophy, which consisted of a small bore/long stroke configuration, which dated back to Peugeot's Le Mans entries. In addition to the engine issues, the car was not as fast as hoped, and struggled to find speed. Although the AP03 was a sleek looking car, their aerodynamics was in reality a nightmare, making the car difficult to drive.

By the time that the cars rolled out for the first practice in Melbourne, the Prost team were already well behind schedule. The practice sessions were marred by problems in the engine, brakes, gearbox, and the suspension for both Alesi and Heidfeld. Alesi languished around the bottom four during the practice sessions while Heidfeld was 13th in the first session, and 17th in the second. Qualifying was slightly better as Heidfeld did a respectable job getting the reluctant machine into the 13th position, while Alesi would line-up four spots behind his teammate.

Just minutes before the cars would roll off on Sunday; Alesi suffered an engine problem in his primary car, resulting in a last minute switch to the spare. Alesi would start from the pitlane in a machine that was not set up for him. In the race, Alesi suffered yet more problems from his Peugeot engine and retired after only 27 laps, while Heidfeld made it to lap 41 before crashing out.

The next round in Brazil was entered with optimism for Prost. The Interlogos circuit is usually one that is well suited to the Prost cars, and it appeared to be the same when Alesi clocked the 6th fastest time in the first practice session. Heidfeld experienced engine problems and in the morning and gearbox gremlins in the afternoon, resulting in only 19 laps for the young German. In qualifying, Alesi experienced problems that included a billboard falling down and getting in the way of the AP03, and lined up 15th. Heidfeld had to use the spare car after suffering clutch problems with the primary and only managed the 19th fastest speed. The race was a nightmare for both, Alesi retiring after only 11 laps due to electronic failure while Heidfeld had already parked his machine two laps earlier after suffering another let down from the A20.

In San Marino, Alesi would start from 15th while Heidfeld would line-up 22nd and last. Heidfeld got a stop and go penalty on race day for stalling on the start on having to be restarted by his mechanics, only to drop out on a lap 22 when his hydraulics failed with Alesi would suffer the same fate only three laps later.

By the time the British Grand Prix rolled around, severe measurers by the FIA to ensure that no team were illegally using electronic driver aids meant that the electronics package had to be massively revised. Prost had already struggled with their new TAG system, but it was about to get worse. The Prost team had conducted a test the previous week to try out their new electronics package as well as some new aerodynamic pieces, but Alesi had managed only two laps before encountering yet more reliability problems. Heidfeld managed 55 laps on the second day of testing, but overall it was a struggle and they still had not solved their reliability concerns heading into the race weekend. After a trying Friday practice both drivers complained of a lack of performance from the engine, Alesi going as far as saying "I have no speed, no acceleration, in short my car is not at all competitive". Alesi ended the session with a spin, which left the car stuck in neutral. In a wet/dry qualifying session Alesi managed to push his reluctant machine to the 15th fastest time and finished 10th, while Heidfeld would be two places back, complaining of traffic and suffering an engine failure on his final lap. The race would offer little more for the unlucky German, as his car would complete 51 laps before suffering a loss of oil pressure resulting in yet another Peugeot engine failure.

One of the few times that the Prost ever looked competitive came at Monaco. Jean Alesi was 7th quick in both practice sessions and turned in a spectacular performance by being the 7th fastest qualifying despite having an alternator problem that forced him to switch to the spare car. Heidfeld had less luck, being in the bottom four during both sessions, first due to a crash and then when a marshal pushed his car, which is not allowed. He would line-up only 18th on the grid. In the race, Alesi ran comfortably until a transmission problem sidelined him on lap 29, blaming it on the three starts the race had. Heidfeld crashed in the morning warm up and had to take Alesi's spare car, but stayed out of trouble and crossed the finish line in 8th. Little did the Prost team know that it would be the best result all season. After Monaco the Prost team, amidst much inter chaos, announced the departure of Alan Jenkins, with Jean-Paul Gousset, who was head of design at Prost, taking up the position as head of the technical department.

Normally one can expect the Prost cars to at least hold their own in their native France. After all, when the team was known as Ligier they were based next to the Magny-Cours circuit. To add to this, Peugeot had released evolution 4 of their A20 engine, which produced more power through all 7 speeds than the previous version. Alesi ended practice complaining of unusual behavior in the tires, while Heidfeld spent the day testing aerodynamic configurations and setups. In qualifying, Alesi was incredibly aggressive and gave his all, only to end up 18th. Afterward he publicly blamed the engine for its unusual behavior entering and exiting corners and questioning its power output. Peugeot, in return, invited members of the media to the Peugeot headquarters to see the engine run and the actual horsepower numbers it produced. There was also a temporary strike by the Peugeot engineers. Hardly the home Grand Prix Alain Prost was expecting! Although Heifeld was only two spots ahead of Alesi, he was much less critical of the engine and the car. On race day, Alesi limped home 14th after being spun by Heidfeld, while the German was eventually classified 16 after having to make an extra pit stop to refuel the engine air system.

One of the many low points for the team came in Austria. After Alesi could only qualify 17th with Heidfeld lining up 13th, the race was an absolute disaster. With Alesi running a lighter fuel load and closing in on Heidfeld, it was expected that the F3000 Champ would let his teammate by. That is not what happened when, entering the first corner at the 41st lap, Heidfeld came down to block a passing attempt by the Frenchman, sending both cars off the track with pieces of Prost's carbon fiber body work everywhere. Both drivers were upset by this incident, which did not to improve inter-team relations.

Spa was a notable run for the AP03, albeit in changing conditions. Alesi has long been acknowledged as a tremendous wet weather racer and after lining up only 17th on the 4.3-mile track, it was these conditions that gave the veteran a chance to shine. Being the first to come in for dry weather tires, he picked up time on the rest of the field even at one point holding fastest lap of the race. He continued his performance throughout the day and looked set for a finish in the points when a break in the fuel system resulted in yet another break down after 32 laps. Like Monaco, Alesi out performed drivers in better machinery with his relentless driving style. Heidfeld qualified 14th and after a pit stop to put on dry tires, and after blipping the throttle while leaving the pits, he did not wait long enough for the revs to come down, and the first gear broke. After a few laps, the engine was finished.

By now serious questions were being pointed at Peugeot's F1 commitment. Peugeot had a title winning World Rally team that was taking priority of the company's auto racing focus and the general perception was that Peugeot was merely full filling their contract obligations to Prost and would bow out of Formula One at the end of the season. Speculation turned to fact on July 25th, when Peugeot announced they would officially end their Formula One involvement on December 31, 2000. In addition, the French car giant had sold its F1 assets, including all personal, to a Japanese company call Asian Motor Technologies headed by Japanese Hideo Morita, who is the son of the late Sony chairman Akio Morita This firm would continue the progress put forth from Peugeot under the Aisatech banner, this time powering the Arrows Formula One team. Peugeot also took it one step further by ever ruling out a Formula One return when the President of Peugeot, Frédéric Saint-Geours, said the pull out was for good, that he was relieved that the company was on longer in F1, and that the decision had been reached in November, 1999. In addition to the Peugeot announcement, in late August, the Swiss Sauber team announced that it had lured Nick Heidfeld away from the team to drive the Sauber Petronas in the year 2001.

The withdrawal of Peugeot meant that Prost would have to look for an alternative engine supply. Unlike the days when a customer Cosworth awaited any team in need of an engine, Formula One customer engines were now in short supply. Rumors had circulated for some time that Mercedes-Benz was interested in supplying Prost, but these rumors were quickly dismissed when politics from McLaren and Mercedes both came into play. Another option might be Renault, like Peugeot a French automotive giant, who were reentering Formula One after a three-year absence. This too was dismissed when Renault demanded that in exchange for a supply of engines, Prost step down from his position as team principal! Finally Alain was able to come to terms with Ferrari and announce a two-year supply of engines on September 22nd. Ferrari had supplied customer engines to the Sauber team, but taking on two teams would be new to the famous Italian marquee. Prost would have to spend between $22 and $26 million annually for the privilege of using the Ferrari 049 engine, the same engine that would eventually power Michael Schumacher to the 2000 World Championship. In addition, Prost would also being using the same seven-speed box as well as a similar electronics package, switching from the disappointing TAG system to long time Ferrari supplier Magnetti Marrelli.

Just how the Prost team were going to pay for the Ferrari engines came into question two days after the United States Grand Prix at Indianapolis, a race which saw Alesi retiring after 64 laps with engine failure and Heidfeld finishing a respectable 9th when the Gaulioses cigarette brand announced that they would end their partnership with the Prost team at the end of the 2000 season. Gaulioses, along with sister brand Gitanes, had been the title sponsorship of the Prost team since 1997 and also the previous Ligier team. However, this was not surprising and not particularly alarming as the company had not kept up with the financial demands of being a title sponsor in modern day Grand Prix racing, and now the estimated $21.8 million they were spending annually was not enough for Prost to justify the advertising return they were receiving.

It was clear at this time that all resources were being devoted to the Prost-Ferrari AP04 and the team simply wanted the 2000 season over. The final time that the AP03 ran in competition was at the season ending Malaysian Grand Prix on the Sepang Circuit. Alesi and Heidfeld lined up 18th and 19th on the grid and in the race Heidfeld was out before the first lap was completed after a collision with Pedro De La Rosa, while Alesi finished 11th, a lap behind race winner Michael Schumacher. The contract with Peugeot meant that post-season testing would have to be done with their French firm's V10 and Prost would have to wait until January of 2001 to began work with Ferrari.

With no major money heading into the 2001 season, Prost then announced eight days after the end of the season that Brazilian Formula One driver and son of a multi-millionaire Brazilian supermarket guru Abilio, Pedro Dinz had purchased a "significant" stake in the Prost Formula One team. Dinz had driven Formula One cars since 1995, including a stint with the Ligier team, but now would take on a managerial role. Prost also appointed Spaniard Joan Villadelprat as managing director and Frenchman Henri Durand as technical director. In addition, the team would switch to Michelin tires, the French company returning to Formula One after being absent since 1984.

Although no title sponsor was found, Prost did find a secondary sponsor in the form of PSN, or Pan-American Sports Network, a sports network that had intended to buy the Minardi team but had back out. The PSN sponsorship also led to the arrival of former Minardi driver and PSN sponsored driver Gaston Mazzacane from Argentina to fill the second seat alongside Jean Alesi.

When one looks back at the 2000 season, one sees a year in which Alain Prost lost most of his major sponsors, his engine supplier (including a total of 47 engines during the year), a significant portion of his team, and his pride. The media ridiculed him at every turn. The fact that he continued into 2001 shows great determination. Whether the former four times World Champion's vision of running a French Formula One team shows his overwhelming confidence or simply bad courage remains to be seen, however.

Matthew